SkillsWork

Student's Book

Lynda Edwards

Contents

Introduction

A message from the author

I have found in my experience that students enjoy and profit better from lessons where the different skills are linked in the way they are in *SkillsWork*. I know that students also need to learn new vocabulary and practise language in a variety of ways. This all happens much more easily if students are interested and engaged in the topic. This is why I wrote the book and I hope you find it both useful and enjoyable.

What is *SkillsWork*?

SkillsWork is an integrated skills book which is designed to give extra practice in the skills of reading, writing, listening and speaking English. It does this through forty different interesting topics and will provide lots of lively language practice. It can be used alongside a standard coursebook or on its own.

How to use *SkillsWork*

There is no one way to use this book. You can select skills you want to develop or topics that are of particular interest to you.

Each unit has a focus skill as well as vocabulary development which includes phrasal verbs, idioms, word building, etc.

A variety of task types give you the opportunity to learn and use new language in a variety of ways.

The recording script is at the back of the book so that you can review it after the lesson if necessary.

Need some company?

Lead in

Work in pairs. Discuss these questions.

- Do you enjoy spending time alone? Why/Why not?
- What activities do you like to do in your time alone?
- Do you think our desire to be or not to be alone changes with age?

Word work

1 a Work in pairs. Look at the words in the box and find as many words as you can with the same roots. Check in a dictionary.

> solitude
>
> alone   society
>
> company   isolate

b Use words from your list to complete the collocations.

1 _____ beneficiary

2 _____ ward

3 _____ confinement

4 _____ hours

5 keep someone _____

2 a Match the colloquial expressions 1–8 with the meanings a–h.

1	enjoy your own company	**a**	relax
2	bounce ideas off each other	**b**	have jokes with friends
3	chill out	**c**	become more sociable
4	come out of your shell	**d**	don't need other people
5	wallow in self pity	**e**	suggest different ideas
6	lick your wounds	**f**	take time to recover
7	exchange banter	**g**	to contribute
8	chip in	**h**	enjoy feeling badly treated

b Divide the expressions into two categories: *alone* (A) and *with others* (B).

3 Choose four expressions from Exercise 2 and give examples of situations when you might use these expressions.

1 a **Choose the correct alternatives to complete the questions.**

1 What d'you think about *to work / working* from home?

2 How d'you *feel / think* about working abroad?

3 I think that would be really difficult. How *about / for* you?

4 *Don't you / Do you not* think it would be better to go to university?

b  **Listen and repeat.**

2 **Work in pairs. Look at the pictures and discuss the advantages and disadvantages of doing these activities alone. Which activities would you least like to do by yourselves?**

Going it alone

3 **Work in pairs/groups. Discuss these questions.**

- Have you ever shared a room? If you have, what were the pleasures and the problems? If you haven't, would you like to? Why/Why not?

- If you had to share a house or a flat with other people, what qualities would they need to make it a successful arrangement?

- In England today some people prefer to bring up children alone rather than in an unhappy relationship. What do you feel about this?

- What are the positive and negative aspects of being an only child?

Write about it

Choose one of these writing tasks.

1 Imagine you have just started to share a flat with two other people. Write an e-mail to a friend telling him or her about the situation.

2 'It's better to grow up with one happy parent than two unhappy ones.' Discuss.

What's in a **voice?**

Lead in

Work in pairs. Discuss these questions.

- Do you usually remember people's voices?
- Name two voices which impressed you pleasantly and unpleasantly.
- What can you remember about the voices of these people?
  someone in your family
  your first boyfriend/girlfriend
  your best friend when you were younger
  the leader of your country
- Do you change your voice when talking to different people?

Listen

🔘 **2.1** Listen to people reading this sentence in different ways.

'I really enjoyed our conversation.'

Match the adjectives in the box with the speakers 1–6.

gossipy sexy business-like squeaky nasal hesitant

Word work

1 Work in pairs. Are the adjectives in the box positive (+), negative (–) or neutral (0)? Check your answers in a dictionary.

husky smooth high fast sexy clear gentle irritating incomprehensible strongly-accented nasal business-like strong piercing aggressive clipped whining musical sharp hypnotic warm gossipy loud deep soft hesitant friendly squeaky nervous enthusiastic pompous upper class rich

2 Think of celebrities who have voices you can describe with some of the adjectives in Exercise 1. Compare your ideas with a partner.

3 Work in pairs. How many different ways can you say this sentence?

'I'd like to talk about this again tomorrow.'

Choose an adjective from the box in Exercise 1. Your partner must try to say the sentence in that type of voice.

Listen

1 Work in pairs. Discuss these questions. Give reasons for your opinions.

- What sort of things do radio adverts advertise?
- What sort of radio ads do you like or dislike?
- Do you think radio adverts persuade you to buy or do different things?
- Do you think advertising on the radio is an effective way to advertise?

2 Look at these statements about radio adverts. Which ones do you think are most important? Give an example of a radio ad you know that one of the statements describes.

'It should be **amusing**.'

'It should have a catchy **slogan**.'

'It should have a catchy **jingle**.'

'It should be **short**.'

'It should be **clever**.'

'It should feature a **celebrity**.'

3 📀 2.2 Listen to some radio ads and write down information about them under these headings.

advert	product	name	tone
1			
2			
3			
4			
5			
6			

4 Work in pairs. Discuss how successful you think these adverts would be. Give reasons for your opinions.

Write about it

Work in small groups and write a radio advert of your own.

1 Think about these questions when you plan your advert.

- What is the product?
- What are the good points of this product?
- How many people do you need – is it a monologue or a short dialogue?
- Are you going to start with some questions?

2 Write the script and indicate voice tone.

3 Record your advert or read it to the class.

Common
sense

Lead in

Work in pairs. Discuss these questions.

- What's the difference between the words in the box?
- Can you give an example of each?

> superstition   coincidence   luck
> premonition   fate   chance

Read about it

1 Work in pairs. Discuss these questions.

1 Look at the title on page 9. What do you think the text is about?
2 What does *telepathy* mean?
3 Have you had or heard about any telepathic experiences?
4 Do you believe that some people are telepathic?

2 Read the text on page 9 and choose the correct answer a, b or c.

1 Scientists haven't researched the subject because:
a they haven't had the time.
b they thought they couldn't prove coincidence.
c they believed it was unorthodox.
d they haven't been able to understand it.

2 According to the text, Dr Sheldrake:
a only investigates this subject.
b was the first to do work on this subject.
c had to travel widely in his research.
d lost his job because of this research.

3 One of Dr Sheldrake's tests involved:
a people staring at each other.
b someone staring at another person's back.
c one person with his eyes closed.
d people saying when someone was staring at them.

4 Dr Sheldrake believes this ability goes back to early man's need:
a to hunt.
b to see the hunter's eyes.
c to be aware of being hunted.
d to find others.

5 Dr Sheldrake's survey show that:
a sometimes people phone each other at the same time.
b people tell each other their intention to phone.
c two phone calls sometimes happen immediately after each other.
d some people can 'see' the other person intending to call them.

6 Groups of animals:
a follow each other to avoid danger.
b have one which acts as the leader.
c pass on a sense of danger to each other.
d communicate with the hunter.

8

The Sixth Sense

Have you ever had the feeling of being watched – and turned round to find someone staring at you? Have you found yourself staring with idle curiosity at someone until they turn their heads to see who is watching them? Have you ever picked up the ringing phone to find it is someone you have just been thinking about?

The answer to all these questions is most likely to be 'yes'. These are common, everyday sorts of experiences, but ones which have never been investigated scientifically until now, because orthodox science doesn't have the faintest idea how to explain them. So it ignores them or calls them 'pure coincidence' and 'superstition'.

Dr Rupert Sheldrake, a biologist who has pioneered work in this area, believes that not only can they be explained and that another sense does exist – but that the explanations are perfectly simple.

In his book, *The Sense Of Being Stared At*, he writes about his experiments on staring and telephone telepathy. He believes they prove the existence of this other sense which tells us when we are being stared at or who is phoning us and gives us other vital information through telepathy and premonition. He says that this is not in any way 'paranormal'.

It is a normal part of our basic nature that we share with animals.

Sheldrake uses members of the public in his experiments and has a data base of 5,000 experiments. One set of experiments involved groups of friends and school mates. One person was blindfolded and sat in front of a 'looker'. The person had to guess when the 'looker' was staring at him. The results were 60% successful – much more than chance would allow. Sheldrake's surveys also showed that 80% of people had had the 'I am being stared at' experience. The great majority of starers turned out to be strangers.

'This must go back to the times when our ancestors were hunted by predators, who of course were strangers,' says Sheldrake. 'This obviously helped survival.' Hunters today also report how animals often show acute awareness they are being stalked even from far away.

Similar to this power of attention is the power of intention which seems to be the cause of telephone telepathy. What is it that tells us that a particular person is going to call us unexpectedly?

Sheldrake believes that before we call we think about it first and this intention reaches out to the person. This is the commonest form of telepathic experience. Over 90% of people in the survey say they have experienced it. Sometimes people find that their calls overlap and the number they are calling is engaged – calling them!

One of the more extraordinary things Dr Sheldrake discovered is that some pets seem to know when someone important to them is about to telephone. Some cats and dogs will go to the phone before it starts to ring. Animal telepathy is a well known phenomenon between social animals who are members of packs, herds, flocks of birds or schools of fish. Obviously, a communicable sense of danger helps them survive predators, keeps them together and allows them to act as one. And when it comes to premonitions – animals beat us hands down! Earthquakes, avalanches and other natural disasters all set off advance fear behaviour in animals, both wild and domestic.

Sheldrake believes this sort of telepathy is a result of mental fields which extend beyond the brain and interact with other people's mental fields. We may be on the edge of a great step forward by understanding how our minds can reach out and touch others at a distance.

Talk about it

Work in pairs. Discuss these questions.
Give reasons for your answers.

- Do you agree with Dr Sheldrake's ideas?
- Do you think twins have a telepathic link?
- Do you think dreams or people can foretell the future?
- Do you think people can be hypnotised to remember previous lives?
- Do you think there is such a thing as real 'magic'?

Useful language
thought-provoking   total rubbish
a ridiculous notion
there's always the possibility
not to be taken seriously
It bears thinking about.   Who knows?
I'd like to keep an open mind on the subject.
You can't prove it one way or another.
There must be something in it.

Write about it

Choose one of the points you discussed and write a paragraph, giving your opinion.

Life in the fast lane

Lead in

Work in pairs. Look at the activities in the box and discuss the questions.

| eat   speak   walk   read   text   make decisions   drink   go to sleep   drive   type |

- How fast do you do these activities?
- Does the speed or slowness of how you do these activities ever cause you problems?
- Are you impatient with people who do things more slowly than you?
- Are you antagonistic towards people who do things more quickly than you?

Word work

1 Match words from A with words from B to make collocations related to driving. Check the collocations in a dictionary.

A

impose   flout   break   drive   enforce
speed   ignore   lower   put your foot on
be inconsiderate to

B

the speed limit   fines/penalties   cameras
the gas   road users   recklessly   the law

2 a Choose three of the collocations from Exercise 1 and write three sentences to show the meanings.

b Work in pairs. Write out your sentences with gaps for the collocations. Exchange your sentences and complete them.

Write about it

1 Work in pairs. Read the text and discuss these questions.

- What problems do you think the residents are experiencing?
- What solutions might there be to the problem?

A local problem

Motorists using the straight stretch of the A352 between Manor Croft and Toll Corner are constantly driving well over the speed limit. This is causing problems for residents who live along and close to the road.

2 Look at the survey results and comments. Use the words in the box to write sentences about the information given.

> the vast majority   many people are worried that   although   whereas   a minority feel   residents commented that   however

Survey Results

Suggested solutions to problems of speeding

Lower the speed limit	42%
Put in speed cameras	85%
Raise speeding fines	81%
Introduce a traffic calming scheme	29%
Have more police patrols	27%
Put in an artificial bend in the road	31%
Put in pedestrian crossings	55%
Withdraw licences	15%

> It can take fifteen minutes to cross the road sometimes.

> There's bound to be a nasty pile up before long. Do we have to wait for that?

> It's impossible to get out of my drive in the mornings! It's taking my life in my hands!

> You sometimes get these fast sports cars racing each other because the road's so straight.

3 Complete the sentences 1–6 using the information in the survey and the words in the box.

> major   number   shows   people
> clear   according

1 Our survey …
2 … to our survey …
3 It is … from our survey …
4 The … surveyed …
5 A … of those questioned felt that …
6 A … point commented on was …

4 You are on a local community committee and have been asked to write a letter to the council. Use the information and comments in Exercise 2 to write the letter.

Divide your letter into the following paragraphs. Work in pairs and discuss what you will include in each paragraph. Then write the letter. Remember to use language appropriate to a formal letter.

1 state the problem and your reason for writing
2 indicate why people are worried
3 summarise the results of the survey
4 conclude with hopes that action will be taken

Talk about it

Which quotation do you agree with? Work in pairs and discuss your ideas.

'**It takes all the running you can do to stay in the same place.**'

(The Red Queen, *Alice through the Looking Glass*)

'**Slow down, you move too fast. You've got to make the morning last.**'

(popular song)

Dress to impress

Lead in

Work in pairs. Discuss these questions.

- Are you image conscious?
- Do you follow fashion or have you developed your own style?
- Who are your favourite designers?
- What do you think your appearance tells people about you?

Word work

Look at the adjectives to describe clothes and situations in the box. Answer the questions.

formal	appropriate	suitable
acceptable	offensive	respectful

1 What are the opposites of these adjectives?
2 What nouns can we make from them?

Talk about it

1 **Work in pairs. Discuss these questions. Use the words in the box to help you.**

   1 What is a dress code?

   2 What do you think the dress code is or should be for the places/situations in the box? Use words from Word work in your discussion.

   Useful language
   a wedding   a night club
   a top restaurant   working in a bank
   teaching   a university   a funeral
   a family celebration   a beach
   shopping   a church   a party

2 **Match these requests with some of the places/situations in Exercise 1.**

   1 no topless sunbathing

   2 no bare chests

   3 no jeans or trainers

   4 black tie

   5 fancy dress compulsory

3 a Match words 1–5 with words a–e to make collocations.

1	feel	**a**	entry
2	not observe	**b**	it completely wrong
3	be refused	**c**	like a sore thumb
4	stick out	**d**	the dress code
5	get	**e**	overdressed

b Have you ever experienced any of the situations or do you know someone who has? Tell your partner about the situation.

4 Work in pairs. Read the situations 1–5 and discuss what you think about what happened to the people. Use the expressions to help you.

1
A young woman whose arms were completely covered in tattoos had an office job. She agreed to keep her arms covered. One day it was very hot and she passed out from the heat. She took off her jacket. She was sacked for exposing her tattoos.

5
Holiday makers walking along Bournemouth beach have complained for many years about the naturist section of the beach. The naturists are still allowed to occupy this section of beach.

2
Customers complained about the lip and tongue piercings of one of the cashiers. He was later dismissed.

3
A young girl was sent home from school for wearing religious headwear because it was not part of the school uniform.

4
A streaker interrupted play at Wimbledon and ran round the court several times before he was caught. He was fined £100.

There's no way they should have …

It was the right thing to do …

It's outrageous!

I'd have let it go.

I'd have done the same.

That was seriously out of order.

That's completely understandable.

Why shouldn't they/he/she?

Life's too short to worry about things like that!

Write about it

Choose one of the situations and write a letter of complaint or support to the appropriate person/company.

It's good to gossip

Lead in

Work in pairs. Discuss these questions.

- What is *gossip*?
- Do you think men and women gossip about the same things?
- How common do you think gossip is?
- How much of your time do you spend gossiping?
- What is your attitude to gossip?

Word work

1 **Match the speakers 1–6 with the colloquial expressions in the box. Sometimes there is more than one answer. Check your answers in a dictionary.**

make small talk   sweet talk   whinge   go on and on   diss
go off on one   have a natter   flatter   moan about

1 I'll do all your laundry for a month if you say yes!

2 The film was rubbish, the coffee was cold and it was freezing in the cinema.

3 He has no tact at all when he's talking to people.

4 I cannot believe he did that to you. Wait till I see him! My brother is the biggest cheater on this planet and I'm sick of him thinking he can just treat every girl he goes out with so badly. You wait till I tell Mum about this latest incident.

5 Weather's brilliant again, isn't it? What did you get up to yesterday then?

6 You're about the most intelligent guy I've met in years. A first from Cambridge – that's amazing. Tell me about your research in that lovely Ferrari of yours.

2 6.1 **Listen and mark the words that are stressed in Exercise 1. Then listen again and repeat.**

3 **Work in pairs. Give your partner a verb from the box in Exercise 1. He/She must talk for 30 seconds in the manner of the verb.**

4 Replace the underlined words with expressions from the box.

1 She's really vicious. She's always <u>saying things that aren't true</u>.

2 <u>People are saying</u> that they're going to close the school.

3 If I tell you what I'm planning you must promise <u>not to tell anyone</u>.

4 <u>Not everyone knows yet</u> but I've been given promotion!

5 There are going to be some big changes in the next few months. Just <u>listen carefully to what's going on</u>.

6 You shouldn't really talk about him <u>when he's not here</u>.

> to keep it to yourself
> spreading rumours
> a rumour's going round
> behind his back
> keep your ear to the ground
> it's not public knowledge

Listen

1 a You are going to hear two people discussing a book called *Gossip is Good for You*. What do you think the interviewer and the author might talk about?

b 🔘 6.2 Listen and check your ideas.

2 🔘 6.2 Listen to the conversation again and decide whether the statements are true (T) or false (F).

1 The interviewer thinks most people agree with her guest.

2 People at the radio station never talk about their boss.

3 The writer thinks it can be good to say bad things about people.

4 Gossiping is quite a new activity.

5 Gossiping can make you feel physically better.

6 Women gossip more than men.

3 🔘 6.2 Listen again and choose the correct alternatives.

1 About *five/fifteen* percent of gossip is negative.

2 When we gossip we exchange *sociable/social* information.

3 We get an important *feeling-/feel*-good factor from gossip.

4 Endorphins are a *natural/naturist* painkiller.

5 Men usually *defy/deny* that they gossip.

4 Do you believe what the writer says? Work in pairs and discuss your ideas.

5 🔘 6.3 Look at the phrases in the box for giving and responding to information. Listen and <u>underline</u> the phrases that are used.

> Did you know …?   You're joking!
> What about the school secretary then?
> It's a wind up!
> You'll never guess what/who …!
> No way!
> Have you heard about …?
> You're having me on!
> Don't tell anyone, but …
> It was only a matter of time.
> This is between you and me, OK?
> That doesn't surprise me.
> Any goss on …?   Give me a break!
> What's the latest on …?

Write about it

Work in pairs and invent a rumour. Choose one of these situations or invent one.

- an interesting fact about a celebrity couple

- an interesting fact about the college or place you are studying in

- an interesting fact about a member of the royal family

- an interesting fact about a local restaurant

Write a short dialogue about the rumour. Use some of the phrases on this page.

THE FOOTBALLER AND THE FILM STAR…
IN FLAGRANTE DELIFTO!
I saw them myself, he was getting her to

Born or made?

Lead in

1 Work in pairs. Discuss these questions.

- What is the meaning of the word *entrepreneur*?
- Can you name a famous entrepreneur? What do you know about him/her?
- What do you think makes a successful entrepreneur?

2 What do you think these sayings mean? Do you agree with them?

1 You make your own luck.

2 Don't complain that life is unfair: get used to it.

3 Be in the right place at the right time.

4 Nothing ventured nothing gained.

5 You should always play by the rules.

Word work

1 The words and phrases in the box are often used to describe successful entrepreneurs. Discuss what you think they mean and check your ideas in a dictionary.

> ruthless   obsessive   charismatic
> competitive   intense   driven   focused
> passionate   dynamic   insatiable
> a risk taker   a control freak   has tunnel vision
> controversial   sociable   easily bored   tough

2 Choose five of the items in the box in Exercise 1 and name a person who can be described in this way. Give a reason for each description. Do any of them describe you?

Read about it

1 You are going to read an article about entrepreneurs. Before you read the article, look at the questions. Work in pairs and discuss possible answers.

1 Which three famous entrepreneurs are mentioned in the article?

2 How much did one business tycoon spend on a birthday party in Cyprus?

3 How much (what percentage) does genetic make up contribute towards our becoming entrepreneurs?

4 Which famous entrepreneur dropped out of university?

2 Quickly read the article on page 17 and check your answers to Exercise 1.

GENES, LUCK AND HARD GRAFT

A Fancy following in the footsteps of Bill Gates and making a billion dollars or so in the computer industry? Or is starting an airline company with a sideline in holiday trips to Space more your line, like Sir Richard Branson of Virgin fame? Well, sorry to disappoint you, but according to recent research, unless you've got the right genes you may as well give up now.

B Entrepreneurs are vital to the economy, increasing wealth and employment. However, the magical quality that separates the employed from the successfully self-employed has so far eluded discovery. What is it that the successful entrepreneur has that the rest of us don't? Is it the type of education, maybe family influence and encouragement? Is it intelligence? Or is it simply luck – being in the right place at the right time?

C Recent research suggests that it's all down to the genes. There have been a series of studies on identical twins (who share the same gene codes) and it appears that the likelihood of our becoming successful entrepreneurs is fifty percent dependant on our genetic make up. Apparently we are born with that drive, determination and other characteristics that can turn us into a retail tycoon like Philip Green (who has made so much money he could afford to spend £5 million on his birthday party in Cyprus).

D Of course, the other fifty percent is made up of useful influences and interestingly, what is called 'random life events'. These are such things as chance encounters, being made redundant or (surprise, surprise!) a lottery win. So it seems that luck does play its part. It also goes without saying that a lot of success is down to hard graft. Do you know of any successful entrepreneurs who worked nine to five?

E Another common denominator is how these guys at the top actually started out. Most didn't have significant academic success and many dropped out of school, college or university to start their own small businesses. Richard Branson started at sixteen, Philip Green dropped out of school at fifteen and a certain Bill Gates dropped out of university to start his own small software company.

So if you've got the right combination of genes, luck and graft – what are you waiting for?

3 Read the article again and answer the questions.

1 Why are entrepreneurs important?

2 Which people were studied in the research and why?

3 What sort of luck is also important for success?

4 What is similar about the way many entrepreneurs started out?

4 Look at the highlighted words in the text and use the context to guess the meanings.

5 Find words or phrases in the article with these meanings.

1 not your main business (A)

_____

2 doing the same as (A)

_____

3 very important (B)

_____

4 It's obvious (D)

_____

5 meetings (D)

_____

6 also contributes (D)

_____

7 left a course before it was finished (E)

_____

Talk about it

Work in pairs. Discuss these ideas.

- Some people say our upbringing plays more of a part in our personality development than our genetic make up. What do you think?

- Science can manipulate genes today. Do you think a parent should be able to choose genetic intervention to control these things?

  sex   health   appearance   intelligence

Write about it

Choose one of these tasks and write a short article.

1 Describe a famous entrepreneur from your country, saying how and why he/she became famous.

2 Describe an imaginary entrepreneur.

Include these points.

- who this person is and what he/she does
- how this person started
- what this person is doing today
- what qualities this person has
- whether or not you admire this person and why

Have your say

Lead in

Work in pairs. Discuss these questions.

- What sort of things might ordinary people want to change in their community or country?
- What can people do to influence these changes?

Word work

1 Match words 1–8 with words a–h to make expressions. Have you ever done or would you ever do any of these things?

1	sign	**a**	with likeminded people
2	go on	**b**	a campaign for/against
3	get in touch	**c**	to newspapers
4	lobby	**d**	a petition
5	post your opinions	**e**	a protest march
6	organise	**f**	online chat with a politician
7	write a letter	**g**	your local MP
8	have an	**h**	on the net

2 a Complete the comments 1–12 with words from the box.

less	pointless	bother	apathetic	silent	along
make	leave	done	bit	cares	feelings	point

1 'One person can't _____ a difference.'

2 'What's the _____?'

3 'It's time the _____ majority spoke up.'

4 '_____ it to the politicians. They know what they're doing.'

5 'I'll go _____ with whatever you decide.'

6 'Why _____. It's _____.'

7 'If everyone thought like you, nothing would ever get _____.'

8 'I couldn't care _____.'

9 'People are so _____ these days.'

10 'No one else _____. Why should I?'

11 'If everyone did their _____, we could really change things.'

12 'We need to make our _____ known, if just for our own conscience.'

b 🔘 **8.1** **Listen and check your answers. Then repeat the comments to practise pronunciation.**

3 🔘 **8.1** **Listen again and decide whether the speakers in Exercise 2 sound concerned (C) or unconcerned (U). Which attitudes best reflect your opinions about people and change?**

Write about it

1 **There are many websites where people can post their opinions on current events or things that concern them.**

Work in pairs. Choose one of the topics and write a conversation to discuss it. Use some of the expressions in the box to comment on your partner's ideas.

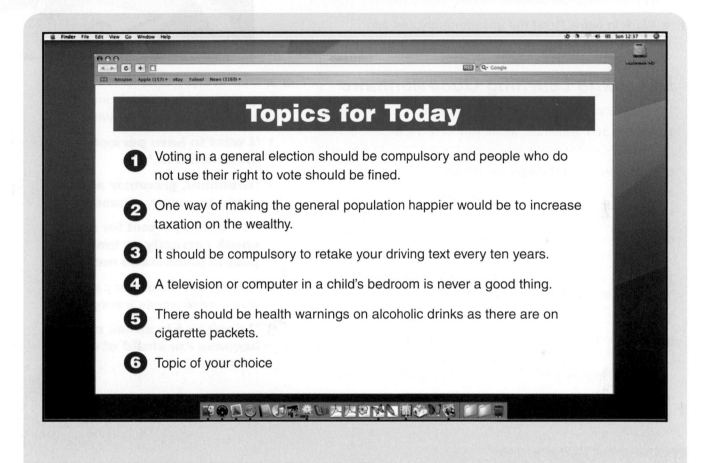

Topics for Today

1 Voting in a general election should be compulsory and people who do not use their right to vote should be fined.

2 One way of making the general population happier would be to increase taxation on the wealthy.

3 It should be compulsory to retake your driving text every ten years.

4 A television or computer in a child's bedroom is never a good thing.

5 There should be health warnings on alcoholic drinks as there are on cigarette packets.

6 Topic of your choice

2 **Look at the conversation you have written and write a comment based on this to post on the website noticeboard. Think about these things.**

- Will your language be formal or informal?
- Will you use paragraphing?

Example:
My friend and I both feel that …
I feel that … but my friend disagrees …

Write about it

Work in pairs. Discuss these questions.

- Do you often complain about things? If so, do you feel better afterwards?

- Should people be able to use the idea of 'freedom of speech' to say anything they like in public, even if it offends others?

Mind your language

Lead in

1 a Work in pairs. Read the questionnaire and add two questions of your own.

Language Learning Questionnaire

1 At what age did you start learning English?

2 What do you remember about your first English classes?

3 What were the first things you learned?

4 What do you remember about your first teacher?

5 Did you enjoy your first language learning experiences?

6 What do you think is the best age to start learning another language? Why?

7 What do you think children should learn first when they start learning another language? Why?

8 _____

9 _____

b Answer the questionnaire and discuss your answers.

2 a Look at these comments about language learning. Which ones do you agree/disagree with? Why?

1 'I want to have perfect pronunciation.'

2 'Grammar, grammar and more grammar, please.'

3 'It's not important for me to speak correctly as long as people understand me.'

4 'I read the dictionary and learn new words everyday.'

5 'I don't like to speak much because I'm afraid of making mistakes.'

b Write two comments that are true for you.

Word work

1 Match words 1–12 with words a–l to make collocations. Compare your answers with a partner.

1	provide	a	advantage of
2	benefit	b	discipline
3	offer	c	your confidence
4	take	d	ample opportunity for
5	focus	e	the risk of
6	tailor	f	bad habits
7	build	g	from
8	pick up	h	a routine
9	self	i	on
10	establish	j	yourself in
11	immerse	k	a course
12	run	l	made

2 Work in pairs. Decide how the different collocations in Exercise 1 could be used to talk about language learning and language learning courses.

Read about it

1 **Look at these adverts for different language courses. Match the first lines 1–7 with the adverts A–G.**

1 Spend your holidays doing something really useful.

2 Learn while you earn!

3 Take advantage of our special in-house training scheme.

4 Study English at a time and place convenient to you.

5 Start them young!

6 No time or money to study English full time?

7 Learn English while you commute.

A
_____

English is important to our company. Improve yours by signing up now for the new release scheme. The first twenty applicants will have two full days' English tuition a month. This will take place in small groups in Room 114 on the first two Fridays of every month. Sign the list now to be assured of a place.

B
_____

The earlier the better. Bring your kids along to our English Fun group every Wednesday at 3.30 in the Diana Room at Kingsford Library. Ages from 4 to 6. You might learn something yourself! Cost £5 per session.

C
_____

Get a job at one of our prestige hotels in the south of England and immerse yourself in the English language. Definitely the best way to learn! Application details: **www.hotelcateringwork.com**

D
_____

Put that time to good use. Our new Audio English Language Course can be used anywhere at any time, even just before you go to sleep!

Learn English within weeks with our carefully programmed package.

E
_____

We offer three and four week intensive courses at schools in three centres just outside London. These courses run throughout the summer and whatever your level we have the appropriate group for you. **Phone for more information: 0621 799732**

F
_____

I am an experienced and well-qualified English Language teacher and I can give you a course of one-to-one lessons tailor-made to your English language needs. Whether you can afford one hour a day or one hour a month, I can design a programme specifically for you. **Contact Sarah on: 07333 46692**

G
_____

Come along to our new English Language evening classes at Collingwood Adult Education College. It doesn't matter whether you want to improve your English to use on holiday or take some exams at the end of the course, we have the course for you – and it won't break the bank. *Pick up one of our brochures for more information.*

2 **Work in pairs. Talk about the advantages and disadvantages of learning English in the situations in Exercise 1. Decide which would be the most effective. Use the phrases in the box to help you.**

Useful language

On one hand … There again … Compared with …
Whereas … It's all very well to … but …
I can see how that might suit some people but …
If you're going for … then …
That wouldn't be right for everyone …

Write about it

Work in pairs. Design your own language course. Decide what your course offers and write the advert for it. Think about these things.

- focus
- cost
- where and when
- reasons to choose this course

Smile please

Lead in

Work in pairs. Discuss these questions.

- Do you usually show your feelings?
- How important do you think it is to smile a lot?
- Which jobs or professions need people to be cheerful all the time?
- How easy is it for you to fake an emotion or hide your feelings?
- Do you think showing or not showing emotion can be a national characteristic?

Word work

1 Divide the text in the box into different expressions.

> he's an old misery guts she's a right whinger her smile lights up her face put a brave face on it grin and bear it keep a stiff upper lip he's always so grumpy she moans all the time he has this cheesy grin it's such a fixed smile she's really gloomy he's got such a long face

2 Work in pairs. Look at the expressions in Exercise 1 and answer the questions.

1 Which expression is positive?

2 Which expressions are about complaining?

3 Which expressions are about covering up sadness?

4 Which expressions are about artificiality?

Talk about it

1 a Work in pairs. Practise saying the expressions in the box. Put as much feeling into them as possible.

Cheer up!
Why should I?

Look on the bright side!
There isn't one.

It can't be that bad!
On no?

It's not the end of the world!
What do you know about it?

I know how to put a smile on your face!
And I know how to take the smile off yours!

b 10.1 Listen and repeat the expressions. Pay attention to the intonation.

2 Work in pairs, Student A and Student B.

Student A: you are very gloomy and refuse to be cheered up.

Student B: you are determined to cheer Student A up.

Roleplay these situations, or situations of your own. Use the expressions in Exercise 1 to help you.

Student A has:

- split up from his/her boy/girlfriend.
- failed his/her driving test.
- not got the job he/she wanted.
- lost his/her mobile phone.

Listen

1 Work in pairs. What do you think these expressions mean? Discuss your ideas.

have a nice day syndrome	emotional labour

2 🔘 **10.2** Listen to a conversation between two friends and complete the sentences.

1 Kelly is happier speaking to Bev because she can _____.

2 When Bev doesn't understand what Kelly's talking about, she say that she's _____.

3 At work Kelly has to _____ to be happy.

4 When Kelly wasn't smiling enough, her boss _____.

5 After a day of smiling at the office, Kelly often _____ on her husband Tom.

3 🔘 **10.3** Listen and repeat the responses. Pay attention to the intonation.

1 Now you really have lost me!

2 OK.

3 You weren't!

4 It's crazy!

5 Tell me about it!

4 Work in pairs. What do you think about the topic the women are discussing? Do you agree with them? Why/Why not?

5 🔘 **10.4** Listen to two more people discussing the issue and answer the questions.

1 What do you think the relationship is between them?

2 Who do you think the people are and where might they be?

3 How is this conversation different from the conversation in recording 10.3?

6 🔘 **10.4** Listen again and decide if the statements are true (T) or false (F).

1 Emotional labour is recognised as an actual condition.

2 People 'fake' emotions when they are tired.

3 People have to be happy in many different roles.

4 People don't need to show their emotions.

5 People worry about what people think of them.

Talk about it

🔘 **10.4** Work in pairs, Student A and Student B.

Student A: take notes of what the man says in recording 10.4.

Student B: take notes of what the woman says in recording 10.4.

Discuss the subject, supporting the view of the speaker whose notes you have.

Write about it

1 Work in pairs. Think up a new slogan for a T-shirt using the word *smile*.

2 Write an e-mail to Kelly. Tell her about the discussion you heard on the radio.

Something must **be done**

Lead in

1 a Look at the photos. How do you think the two things might be connected?

b Scan the article to check your ideas.

The Peacock and the Petrol Pump

A In springtime should you wish to fill up your car at a popular Total filling station in The Forest of Dean, Gloucestershire, you may well have to dodge a resplendent peacock to get to the pump. Mr P (as he is known) has fallen in love with the pumps and everyday he struts the quarter of a mile from his home on a local estate where he lives with his two brothers, to get to the station. There he spends up to eighteen hours a day courting the objects of his affection.

B It is thought that Mr P has mistaken the clicking noise of the pumps for the mating cry of a peahen. He may also be attracted by the bright red and white colours. Whatever the reason, poor Mr P has got the love bug badly and needless to say the pumps do not feel the same way. Unfortunately for Mr P, peacocks are territorial and once attracted will return again and again, whether or not their love is reciprocated.

C The staff at the station have become quite attached to Mr P and feel sorry for him as he struts his stuff around the pumps, displaying his wonderful plumage all to no avail. Most customers are also quite taken by the unusual sight and Mr P has become a minor tourist attraction in the area.

D Unfortunately not everyone is happy to have a love-struck peacock in the vicinity. Some local residents are disturbed by the screeching. There have been many complaints to the local council and it seems that Mr P's days of serenading the pumps may well be numbered. It has been suggested that he is taken far away to be released into the wild, well away from the clicking loves of his life.

2 Read the article again and decide if the statements are true (T) or false (F).

1 Mr P sometimes gets in the way.

2 Peacocks often go back to the same places.

3 Mr P is unpopular with the staff.

4 People who live nearby enjoy the sound he makes.

5 Mr P can definitely stay at the garage.

Word work

1 Find words and phrases in the article to match these words and phrases.

1 move around something (A) _____

2 wonderful to look at (A) _____

3 feathers (C) _____

4 near them (D) _____

5 high-pitched noise (D) _____

6 probably won't last long (D) _____

2 Without looking back at the article, try to complete the expressions.

1 the _____ cry of a peahen

2 a love _____ peacock

3 He's got the love _____ badly.

4 Most customers are quite _____ by the unusual sight.

5 The staff have become quite _____ to Mr P.

3 a The verbs in the box are usually used with animals. Do they refer to sound (S) or movement (M)?

strut   roar   bark   screech   yelp   pounce   growl
purr   trot   squeak   hover   hiss   soar

b Which animals are the verbs usually associated with?

3 Complete the sentences with the correct form the verbs in Exercise 3.

1 I was trying to talk to Zoe but the boss was _____ in the background.

2 The manager _____ on every mistake I make. He wants me out.

3 He _____ around the office as if he owns the place.

4 Last months our sales figures _____.

5 'I adore you,' she _____.

6 The army sergeant _____ his orders at the men.

Talk about it

1 Work in pairs. Discuss what reasons the residents might have for complaining about the peacock.

2 Role play a phone conversation made by one of the residents to the local council to complain. Here are some expressions you can use in your conversation.

Resident
This is the fifth time I've …
We want some action.
This is ruining our lives.
We're not going to take this lying down.
You people need to get your act together!
Can't you do anything?
What are you going to do about it?
This is just not good enough.
If you were in our shoes …
I'm not the only one complaining …

Councillor
Your complaint has been noted.
It has been passed on to the proper department.
We are currently dealing with your complaint.
I'm afraid there is nothing we can do.
We appreciate your situation.
This is a difficult situation for all involved.

3 Look at the Resident's expressions in Exercise 2. Think of formal equivalents for each one. Use the phrases in the box to help you.

Useful language
take some action   in our situation   not alone
unbearable   continue to pursue this matter
steps you can take

Write about it

Write a letter of complaint to the council. Divide your letter into these sections.

- say who you are and why you're writing
- describe the situation you are complaining about.

- request action
- say what you intend to do if no action is taken

Great British **food**

Lead in

1 Work in pairs. Discuss these questions.

- What is the reputation of British food in your country?
- What do (did) you think British people like to eat?
- Have you tried any British food? What? What was your reaction?
- Is there anything you would like to try? What? Why?

2 Match the dishes in the box with the pictures 1–4. Would you like to try these dishes? Why/Why not?

> Yorkshire pudding   spotted dick
> star gazey pie   bangers and mash

Read about it

1 Read the advert for a new restaurant. Which statement is not true?

1 The meals aren't too expensive.
2 You can try international dishes.
3 The atmosphere and décor are amazing.

DON'T MISS THE GASTRONOMIC EXPERIENCE OF A LIFETIME AT

❧ The Best of British ❧

This wonderful new restaurant will be opening
on 8th July in Marlands Court and offers real traditional
British food at affordable prices in a glorious setting.
No pasta, no curries, no snails or chilli peppers!
Fresh tasty ingredients cooked by a master chef
will tantalise your tastebuds and reacquaint
you with the food of your heritage.

Book now to avoid disappointment. 01257 87132

---

2 Complete the sentences with the correct words.

> high   meet
>
> low   (expectations)   fall short
>
> come up to   surpass

1 If you have _____ expectations, you are never disappointed!
2 My mother's expectations are always so _____ nothing ever _____ them.
3 We hope a visit to our restaurant will not only _____ all your expectations but _____ them!
4 When I was a child I always _____ of my parents' expectations.

26

The 'Best of British' is the best!

I was (1) _____ to last night's grand opening of the controversially named 'Best of British' restaurant and I have to (2) _____ that I attended the event with some (3) _____ and fairly low expectations. I had (4) _____. of my stomach being assaulted by the stodgy puddings and bland vegetables of my schooldays. In my experience the British are much better at eating food (note expanding waistlines) than they are at cooking it. And after all, what is British cooking? Fish and chips and mushy peas? So, while not actually quaking in my boots, I did have a packet of indigestion tablets in my back pocket.

I couldn't have been more (5) _____. I take (6) _____ everything I have ever said about British cooking. We were (7) _____ to a five-course meal of absolute perfection.

The (8) _____ began as soon as we entered the stylish, air conditioned restaurant. Delicate aromas designed to whet the appetite drifted across the spacious dining room. You immediately felt that you were somewhere special. The décor is, as described in the advertisement, simply glorious. Nothing is cramped or quaint or countrified. The room is high ceilinged and glamorously decorated in the style of the 1940s. Crisp, white tablecloths and exquisite cutlery and crockery dress the tables and elegant, discreet waiters hover unobtrusively. I was glad I had (9) _____ for the occasion. Jeans would have definitely been out of place here!

The menu was an (10) _____ in itself. There was a wonderful variety of dishes from many regions of the British Isles with information about their origins and the traditional ways of cooking them. Then the food arrived. It was simply to (11) _____ for! Mouth-watering, melt-in-your-mouth pies, smoked meats and fish, lightly steamed puddings, roast game and all (12) _____ by fresh, beautifully cooked seasonable vegetables and delicate sauces that (13) _____ the main food items perfectly. The desserts reminded me of Sundays in my gran's kitchen when I was a child. Steamed treacle pudding, custard tart, strawberry shortcake and summer pudding, topped with clotted cream from Devon were all there on the menu. As well as tasting delicious, the food was beautifully presented. A complete feast for the senses.

Eating at the 'Best of British is a gastronomic experience. I would most definitely (14) _____ it. It certainly lived up to the (15) _____. A little heavy on the wallet but definitely not heavy on the stomach.

---

3 Read the restaurant review and complete the text with words from the box.

> treated   apprehension   mistaken   complemented
> dressed   invited   die   admit   visions   hype   education
> recommend   back   experience   accompanied

4 a Find the nouns that are described with these adjectives.

1 stodgy _____   5 smoked _____

2 bland _____   6 gastronomic _____

3 mouth-watering _____   7 roast _____

4 steamed _____   8 seasonable _____

b Work in pairs and test each other. Take it in turns to say an adjective. Can your partner supply the noun?

5 Find words or phrases from the unit that you could use to describe these aspects of a new restaurant.

> expectations   décor   menu   food   recommendation

Write about it

1 Work in pairs. Write an advert for the opening of a new restaurant. It can be any type of restaurant. Use the advert on page 26 as a guide and use a dictionary to help you.

2 Exchange your advert with another pair. Imagine you have visited this restaurant. Make notes using the guide above and then write a review for their restaurant. Remember to structure your review carefully.

- name the restaurant and say when you went there
- describe your expectations.
- describe your experience and comment on what impressed or didn't impress you
- give a recommendation to go or not to go

Get your priorities **right**

Lead in

1 Work in pairs. Read the comments and discuss which one best describes you.

'I always leave the boring stuff till last and then often I don't get round to it!'

'I always do the most important things first – even if they're difficult!'

'I just do things when I think about them.'

'I make lists of things I have to do.'

2 Think of some situations when we have to prioritise. E.g. deciding what is most important to take on holiday.

Word work

1 a Work in pairs. Look at the words in the box and think about how they are used. Answer the questions and check your ideas in a dictionary.

prioritise	choose	select	opt	rank	order

1 Are they formal/informal?

2 In what situations would you use them?

3 Do they have following prepositions?

b How many different words can you make?

2 Use the correct form of the words in Exercise 1 to complete the sentences.

1 I'm afraid I've got no _____ but to cancel the contract.

2 Put these points in _____ of importance.

3 In motor racing he's _____ number one in the world.

4 If you don't like the deal, you can _____ out.

5 The government says that welfare is their top _____.

6 They have an excellent _____ of salads.

7 He's quickly climbed up the world's _____.

8 At a roundabout traffic coming from the right has _____ over that coming from the left.

9 They're very _____ about who they accept as members.

Talk about it

1 What is most important to you in these situations?

Example: Buying new clothes – fashion, comfort, price?

> choosing a career
> buying a new car
> choosing a place to live
> leaving a burning building
> choosing a holiday
> bringing up a child

2 List at least three things that are important for you in each of the situations in Exercise 1. Then work in pairs and compare and discuss your lists.

Listen

13.1 **Listen to a discussion about the news and answer the questions.**

1 Which two news stories are mentioned?

2 Are the man and the woman both from the same country?

3 Who is David Beckham?

4 Why does the woman criticise the news reporting?

Talk about it

1 Work in pairs. Discuss the questions. Use some of the expressions used in recording 13.1.

- How far do you agree with the points made in the recording? Why?

- Are you happy with the priorities given to news reporting in your country? Why/Why not?

- How important is it to include 'happy news items' in news reports?

- How much do computer graphics contribute to news reports?

- Do you think it is important to use graphic images, photos and video footage to accompany certain reports?

> **I can't believe …**
> **Did you realise that …**
> **That's not the point …**
> **I know what you're saying, but …**

2 Work in pairs. Look at the list of news stories and add two more of your own. Decide which order they should appear in for a news bulletin.

1 Big rise in oil prices

2 A report on an international football match

3 Strike by air traffic controllers on the busiest day of the year

4 Soldiers die in war in Middle East

5 Two famous film stars announce they are getting divorced

6 Terrorist attack in your capital city is foiled

7 Drugs related shooting at a night club in your capital city

8 _____

9 _____

Write about it

Choose one of the news stories above and write a short news report on it.

We know what you're **doing**

Lead in

Work in pairs. Discuss these questions.

- How important is privacy to you?
- In your country what sort of information do people usually like to keep private in general conversation?
- In what ways can the authorities keep track of what we've done and what we're doing?
- In your country is information about you easily accessible to others?

Word work

1 Make nouns from the words in the box. Check your answers in a dictionary.

> secure   private   access   identify   secret
> protect   safe   prove   public

2 Choose three words from Exercise 1 and write gap fill sentences. Then work in pairs and complete each other's sentences.

3 Where would you see or hear these sentences? What do they refer to?

1 Trespassers will be prosecuted.

2 Please respect the privacy of the person in front.

3 Your call may be recorded for training purposes.

4 Star seen kissing son's fiancée on private yacht.

4 Complete the collocations 1–8 with the verbs in the box. Sometimes there is more than one possible answer.

> put   tail   trace   invade   bug   steal
> catch   match   respect   track

1 _____ someone on film

2 _____ someone's movements

3 _____ someone's phone

4 _____ a suspect

5 _____ someone under surveillance

6 _____ someone's privacy

7 _____ someone's DNA

8 _____ someone's identity

30

Listen

1 a Work in pairs. Discuss situations when these things might be important.

> phone tapping   CCTV   satellite navigation tracking
> identity cards   DNA test

b Write down three items of vocabulary connected with each one.

2 🔘 **14.1** **Listen and match the speakers A–E with the topics in Exercise 1.**

3 a 🔘 **14.1** **Listen again and match the opinions 1–8 with the speakers A–E.**

1 Things have gone too far.

2 It's a load off my mind.

3 You need strong grounds to do this.

4 It's reassuring.

5 It's the ultimate invasion of privacy.

6 Safety first.

7 Thieves will up their game.

8 The laws are nowhere near tight enough.

b Can you say these expressions in another way?

4 🔘 **14.2** **Listen to the phrases. <u>Underline</u> the words that are stressed. Repeat the phrases with the same word stress.**

A It's just so reassuring to know that I can find out where she is at any time.
It's amazing.
These days it's so important to know where they are and that they're safe
Life is so dangerous these days.

B I can't stand it.
I think it's simply appalling.
You can't go anywhere in this town without being caught on film.
Big Brother is watching us.

C These checks have gone too far.
I mean, photos fine but eye prints? Thumb prints?
And as for having all this information in one place – that's just asking for trouble.

D I totally agree …

E No. I think the laws controlling this are nowhere near tight enough.

Talk about it

Work in groups. Discuss these questions.

- Should adopted children have the right to know the identity of their birth parents?

- Should celebrities have the right to privacy?

- Should governments have the right to test and record the DNA of the entire population?

- How far should government information be accessible to the public?

- Do you think parents ever have the right to read their children's private correspondence?

Write about it

Choose one of the topics on this page and write a letter to a newspaper giving your opinion.

They're out to get us

Lead in

Work in pairs. Discuss these questions.

- In how many different places can we see adverts?
- What form do the adverts take (posters, leaflets, etc.)?
- Do you notice, read and react to visual adverts? Why/Why not?
- What changes have you noticed in visual advertising over recent years?

Read about it

1 Quickly look at text A and text B on page 33 and answer the questions.

1 Where do you think they are from?

2 What differences would you expect to find in the type of language used?

2 a Work in pairs. Look at the words in the box which are taken from the texts and discuss their meanings. Check in a dictionary if necessary.

> inundated   a snippet   exempt   weirder   graft
> subjected to   dangle   fine-tuned   vying for
> grab   high-tech   captive audience

b Which words do you think are from text A and which are from text B?

3 Work in pairs, Student A and Student B.

Student A: read text A.
Student B: read text B.

Ask and answer questions about these things in your texts.

1 where we can see adverts

2 the number of adverts we see

3 what is advertised

4 types of adverts

5 use of technology

A _____

Imagine this: You're on an escalator coming up from the underground system after a hard day's graft. You're tired and just let the escalator carry you up. As you pass the posters on the wall, a message follows you up, changing what you read in each frame.

Or this: You're on the platform going to work and glancing casually at the ads displayed on the tunnel walls opposite. They're advertising a daily newspaper. That evening you're going out again and you're standing in exactly the same place on the same platform. But are you? The advertisement is now for a restaurant. If you'd been there at lunchtime you'd have seen yet another advert for a local sandwich shop.

Even weirder: You stand in front of an advert on the wall and it changes when you move away and someone of a different sex goes to look at it. Other adverts are constantly changing. You count. It's every ten seconds!

Or perhaps you prefer to travel by bus. You're waiting at the bus stop and the advertisement you see displayed suggests that you press the interactive button to bring up information about a particular product. You can ask questions. Or maybe the advert is for a new album and there's a blue tooth connection that lets you download a snippet to listen to.

Perhaps you've sometimes felt that advertising posters are a bit boring and flat. How about an advert for a shoe shop with a virtual shoe hanging in the air that you can view from all angles? It's real, isn't it? What is real is that advertisers will soon be using every possible high-tech advance to grab and keep our attention. Adverts that flash, move, talk, change, follow us, target us, dangle in front of us will haunt our streets and transport systems in the constant battle for our money.

B _____

It is apparently a fact that the number of advertisements we see today in one year is more than our parents would have seen in a lifetime. Advertisers are constantly vying with each other for our attention and continually researching new ways to reach us using the latest technology. Being inundated with over 500 advertisements every day leads us to screen out a large amount so over the next decade we shall be subjected to more and more inventive ways of making us look and keep looking. On the underground, for example, where the advertisers have a captive audience, the adverts will be fine-tuned to the time and place. This means that they will change according to the time of day and the target audience. Interactive adverts encourage an emotional response that makes them memorable and we shall see interactive adverts at places like bus stops where people have the time to investigate. Virtual advertising is much more attractive to the consumer as is video and both will be exploited in the future. Our computers will not be exempt from the advertising invasion. We may well have advertising blocks in place but blogvertising is popular at the moment as is the less creative but extremely effective method of paying search engines to link a company's products with key words so that the advertising really does target the person who might respond.

4 a Work in pairs. Look again at the words in Exercise 2. Can you remember the context they were used in?

b Underline the places they appear in the text.

5 Work in pairs. Read the text you didn't read in Exercise 4. Talk about which text is more formal and why. Think about these things.

- vocabulary
- grammar
- linking expressions and structure

Talk about it

Work in pairs. Discuss these questions.

- What do you think *blogvertising* is?
- Do you think high-tech advertising like this will be a good or bad thing?

- If you had a new product to advertise, which of the ways mentioned do you think would be most effective and why?

Write about it

Write a comment for the *Have Your Say* website on advertising of the future.

For your reference

Lead in

1 a Look at the questions and answer them with a rating of 1–5 (1 = very positive, 5 = very negative).

b Work in pairs. Compare and discuss your answers.

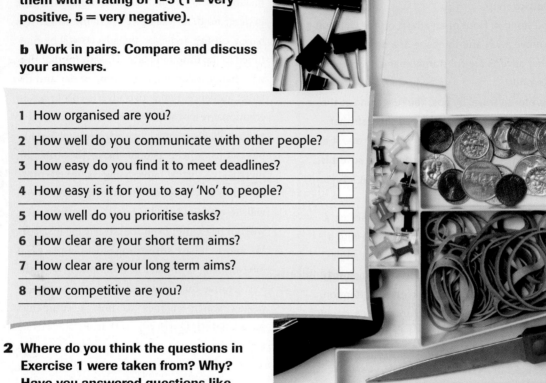

1 How organised are you?	☐
2 How well do you communicate with other people?	☐
3 How easy do you find it to meet deadlines?	☐
4 How easy is it for you to say 'No' to people?	☐
5 How well do you prioritise tasks?	☐
6 How clear are your short term aims?	☐
7 How clear are your long term aims?	☐
8 How competitive are you?	☐

2 Where do you think the questions in Exercise 1 were taken from? Why? Have you answered questions like them in the past?

Word work

1 a Make adjectives from the verbs and nouns in the box. Check your answers in a dictionary.

| rely judge support decide commit trust organise |
| motivate construct invent compete innovate |
| enthusiasm profession access sense person |

b Work in pairs. Take turns to give a definition of an adjective for your partner to guess.

2 Complete the sentences with adjectives from Exercise 1.

1 Criticism is fine, as long as it's _____.

2 Don't wear jeans to work. It doesn't look _____.

3 People like her immediately. She's very _____.

4 We need to know that you are _____ to the company.

Talk about it

Work in pairs. Discuss these questions.

- Which qualities are most important for a successful manager?
- Have you ever written a reference?
- What should a reference include?
- Should you always tell the truth in a reference?

Read about it

1 Read the reference and answer the questions.

1 Do you think the writer of the reference would really recommend May to another employer?

2 What do you think the highlighted phrases really mean?

May Thompson has worked for Trelawney's for three months. She came to us after working for a similar company for ten weeks. I have been her line manager and directly responsible for May's work. Her work is mainly of a secretarial nature and involves inputting data and word processing.

In her time with us, May unfortunately contracted an as yet undiagnosed sporadic virus which caused her to take ten days' sick leave in the period. In addition to this, May's awareness of time is rather erratic and she attributes this to the fact that she doesn't wear a watch because of allergies. May is an extremely sociable girl and she communicates very well with her colleagues, both inside and out of the office. She has an unusual dress sense and an interesting taste in body decoration.

May's computer skills are adequate for the tasks she is employed to do, although unfortunately her particular computer tends to crash quite regularly. May is certainly enthusiastic in voicing her opinions and she is constantly coming up with very innovative suggestions regarding redesigning the workplace. It is true that she could extend to fill several work stations. She likes to bring a significant amount of personal items to work. May's colourful personality would brighten up any office.

For a confidential phone reference, please contact me on:

2 Find words or phrases in the reference with these meanings.

1 been employed by _____

2 during her period of employment _____

3 she came to us _____

4 in her job description _____

5 satisfactory _____

6 concerning _____

7 creative _____

8 the reason she gives is _____

Write about it

Someone who works for you has applied for a higher position with a rival company. Write him/her a reference. Include information on these points.

- punctuality   • dress   • time management   • teamwork   • abilities

Making **money**

Lead in

Work in pairs. Discuss these questions.

- How important is it to have money?
- How much money would you like to have?
- What would you do with a lot of money? How would your lifestyle change?
- How can people make a lot of money?
- How can people make a lot of money quickly?

Word work

1 Match words 1–9 with words a–i to make collocations.

1	invest	**a**	a return
2	break	**b**	profits
3	launch	**c**	ends meet
4	initial	**d**	a backer
5	make	**e**	a new business
6	get	**f**	even
7	projected	**g**	money
8	find	**h**	investment
9	sound	**i**	outlay

2 Replace the underlined words with collocations from Exercise 1.

1 It's a really safe place to put your money.

2 The cost of setting up the business is going to be high.

3 I'll be happy as long as we don't make a loss!

4 We need to get someone to invest in the business.

3 Work in pairs. Take it in turns to supply one part of a collocation from Exercise 1 and see if your partner can complete it.

Listen

1 🔘 17.1 Listen to the conversation and answer the questions.

1 What's the relationship between the speakers?

2 What business does Ruth want to start?

3 Is James going to back her?

2 🔘 17.1 Listen again complete each expression so that it has the same meaning as the one above.

1 someone who will do well in business

have a _____

2 tell me about it

run it _____

3 think about the details of a project

think something _____

4 money spent to keep the business going day to day

running _____

5 discuss money

_____ money

1 **Work in pairs and discuss the questions.**

> What are the advantages and disadvantages of starting a new business?

> What sort of things do you have to think about when starting a new business?

2 **Work in pairs. Look at the expressions in the box and try to think of other ways of saying them. Use your dictionaries if necessary. Practise saying them with the correct intonation.**

Useful language
I have an amazing proposition for you.
We'd be ahead of the field.
We'd rake in the profits.
Do you fancy making a quick buck or two?
It's a completely new concept in …
There's a gap in the market for …
It's just what the market needs.
It's a niche market.

3 **Work in groups divided into As and Bs.**

Student As: You have ideas for new businesses. They can be one of the ones in the box or your own ideas.

| restaurant | health centre | salon | specialist shop | cyber café |

Work together to design a brief business plan. Think about these things.

- what you want to provide
- why you think it will be successful
- what the running costs will be
- what the initial outlay will be
- what competition there is

Student Bs: You are potential investors. Work together to plan questions to ask the different business partners. Think about these things.

| competition | unique selling point | initial outlay |
| running costs | possible return |

4 **Work in pairs of As and Bs. Role play the situation in Exercise 3. Pairs of business partners visit pairs of investors and make their pitch. Each pitch should take five minutes. Continue until all the pairs have met. Then investors decide which business they want to invest in.**

Wired for **sound**

Lead in

1 Work in pairs. Discuss these questions.

- How important is music in your life?
- Where, when and how often do you listen to music?
- What sort of music do you like/ not like listening to?
- Where today can we hear music that we can't control?

2 a Work in pairs. Look at the pictures and answer the questions.

1 What sort of music might we hear in these places and situations?

2 What is the music there for?

3 Do you think it's good to have music in these places? Why/Why not?

b ◎ **18.1** **Listen to reasons for and against having music playing. Were they the same as yours?**

Listen

1 ◎ **18.1** **Listen again and note down the pictures that are mentioned. Which other places are discussed?**

2 Match the comments 1–5 and the places a–e.

1 put you off shopping	a restaurant
2 doze off for a while	b supermarket
3 puts you in a good mood	c hospital
4 actually be good for people	d train
5 it's not completely in your face	e clothes shop

3 ◎ **18.1** **Listen again. Who says these phrases, Simon (S) or Lizzie (L)?**

1 Don't you think

2 So?

3 I suppose it's OK

4 What I don't like is when

5 to be honest

6 nothing's worse than

7 don't knock

8 Seriously, aren't there

9 Apparently,

10 I think you've made your point.

11 You are such a killjoy!

12 You're twisting my words.

4 a Match the beginnings from 1–6 with the endings a–f.

1 What I don't like is …	**a** it's illegal in France.
2 There's nothing worse than …	**b** raising the age for buying cigarettes.
3 Don't knock …	**c** when the phone rings in the middle of the night.
4 Don't you think that …	**d** travelling on a crowded tube train.
5 Apparently, …	**e** the rich should pay higher taxes?
6 They're talking about …	**f** The Rolling Stones.

b 🔘 **18.2 Listen and check. Do you agree with the speakers?
Think of another ending for the phrases in 1–6.**

5 a 🔘 **18.3 Listen and mark the words that are stressed in this dialogue.**

Tony: In my opinion all mobile phones on trains should be banned!

Denise: Well, I think you're in a minority.

Tony: Come on. Some people spend the whole journey with a phone glued to their ear.

Denise: Now you're exaggerating.

Tony: How they can have intimate conversations in front of a carriage full of people is beyond me!

Denise: And I suppose you've never used a mobile on a train?

Tony: Well, emergencies are a different matter.

Denise: Yeah. Like when you called me yesterday to let me know when to start cooking dinner.

**b Work in pairs. Read the dialogue aloud and practise the correct stress
and intonation.**

Talk about it

**Work in pairs and discuss the statement.
Think about these things.**

- where you find street musicians in your country
- why these people play music in the streets
- what nuisance (if any) they present

**'Street musicians
should be banned.'**

Write about it

**Work in pairs. List points for and against the statement and write a dialogue
using as many of the expressions on this page as you can. Practise reading
the dialogue together.**

The hands of **time**

Lead in

Work in pairs. Discuss these questions.

- What do you understand by the word *image*?
- Have you ever deliberately changed your image?
- How do you think our attitude to our image changes throughout our lives?
- Should we be more or less concerned about our appearance as we get older?
- What steps can people take to look after their appearance as they age?

Word work

1 **Look at the sets of words with similar meanings. What are the differences in meaning in each set? Check your ideas in a dictionary.**

| image | appearance | style | look | trend |

| classy | elegant | smart | sleek | arrogant |

| casual | scruffy | cool | laid-back |

2 **Complete the sentences with words from Exercise 1.**

1 A model has to look after her _____ carefully.

2 If you work in business and deal with clients, you have to be _____.

3 If you look _____, you'll be sent home to smarten up!

4 Everything – her clothes, manners, way of walking – make her a very _____ lady.

Read about it

1 **You are going to read an article about cosmetic surgery. Work in pairs. Discuss these questions.**

- What cosmetic procedures do you know of?
- What points do you think may be discussed in the article?

2 **Scan the article on page 41 and tick the procedures that are mentioned**

nose reshaping	ear procedures
eyelid reduction	liposuction	tummy tucks
hair transplants	face lifts	tattoo removals

3 **Complete the article with the best word, a, b, or c. Make sure you know the meanings of all the words.**

	a	**b**	**c**
1	pushes	progresses	advances
2	surgeon	knife	anaesthetic
3	numerous	staggering	high
4	undergoing	going under	undertaking
5	need	queries	demand
6	unmistakable	error free	flawless
7	budget	money	salary
8	fear	shame	anger
9	blow	plump	expand
10	eliminate	eradicate	wipe out
11	obsession	awareness	infatuation

The Hands of Time

Exactly how far will most of us go to look good? The answer seems to be – as far as we can afford and as far as (1) ____ in cosmetic surgery will allow us. According to recent statistics, millions more of us these days are prepared to go under the (2) ____ in the search of continuing youthful appearance and perfection. Figures in the US indicate that there are well over nine million cosmetic procedures every year and in the UK there was a 22% increase last year.

The range of procedures today is quite (3) ____. From face lifts to tummy tucks and nose reshaping to hair transplants, it appears that practically any aspect of our bodies that we would like to be different can be changed. And there is a significant increase in the number of men (4) ____ cosmetic procedures. Apparently, the most common operations for men include nose reshaping, eyelid reduction, corrective surgery for prominent ears and liposuction. For women the most significant recent increase has been a 40% rise in (5) ____ for facelifts and eyelid reductions by older women – the so called 'silver surgery generation'.

In the past only the rich and famous could afford the exorbitant fees demanded to have (6) ____ skin and new noses but it is now well within the (7) ____ of the man (or woman) on the street. New noses in your late teens and a face lift at forty are quite the norm. They are even given as presents to loved ones.

Another change is people's attitudes to cosmetic surgery. Previously those who had undergone the surgery tried to keep it a secret – there was an element of (8) ____ associated with not allowing oneself to grow old gracefully. Being overly concerned with appearance was not something that was talked about. Today both men and women take great pride in their surgery. They can't wait to show off their new look to their friends. It has become quite acceptable for us to attempt to turn back the hands of time.

Of course, surgery is not the only option. There are injections that can (9) ____ up thin lips or paralyse nerves to produce smooth skin. There are fillers to (10) ____ wrinkles, lasers to burn away imperfections and skin can even be rejuvenated with injections of our own cells. And there are the miracle creams that are becoming more and more miraculous and more and more expensive, promising a whole new you within a matter of weeks.

This (11) ____ with looking younger or recreating yourself in your own image is obviously big business for the beauty industry. But I'm sure there are many of us asking – just how long can we keep turning back the hands of time? These procedures do not come with lifelong guarantees. In the end time wins out but just how important is it to keep up the fight?

4 Read the article again and answer the questions.

1 What do these numbers refer to: 9, 40, 22?

2 Does anything in the article surprise you? Why?

3 What does the last sentence mean? Do you agree?

Talk about it

1 a Work in pairs. Discuss these questions and make a note of your ideas.

- Should teenagers be allowed to have cosmetic surgery?
- Do you think this obsession with cosmetic surgery will continue to rise?
- From what you have heard or read, is cosmetic surgery always successful? What are the dangers?
- What is your personal reaction to the topic of cosmetic surgery? Would you have a procedure? What would you change about your body?

b Tell the class your ideas and compare opinions. Make a note of the other opinions in your class.

Write about it

Use the notes you made during the class discussion to write a short summary of the class's attitude to cosmetic surgery. Use some of the expressions in the box.

Useful language
The majority of the class …
Only a few believed …
Over half considered …
supported the idea that …
were in favour of …

Our survey **says**

Lead in

Work in pairs. Discuss these questions.

- Do you often get asked questions for a survey?
- What have you been asked recently and where was the survey being conducted?
- Have you heard of any ridiculous surveys?

Read about it

1 **You are going to look at a survey about working hours across the world. Work in pairs. Ask and answer these questions.**

- How many hours a day/a week do people work on average in your country?
- How many days' holiday a year do people have on average in your country?
- Do you think this amount of time is about right, too little or too much? Why?

2 **Work in pairs. What do you think are the answers to the questions?**

The World at Work

1 a In which country do people work the longest hours per year?
  b How many hours do they work:
    1,957, 2,317 or 3,108?

2 a In which country do people work the shortest hours per year?
  b How many hours do they work:
    1,644, 1,611 or 1,481?

3 a In which country do people take the most annual holiday?
  b How many days to they take:
    35, 30 or 25?

4 a In which country do people take the least annual holiday?
  b How many days do they take:
    9, 10 or 11?

3 **Scan the survey results to check your answers to Exercise 2.**

Working practices across the world

Country	Average hours worked per year	Days of holiday per year
South Korea	2,317	10
Hong Kong	2,231	9
India	2,205	17
Taiwan	2,143	12
USA	1,957	11
Switzerland	1,807	23
United Kingdom	1,782	20
Spain	1,758	22
Italy	1,747	21
Sweden	1,726	25
Luxembourg	1,725	25
Athens	1,714	24
Brazil	1,709	30
Holland	1,687	25
Brussels	1,672	21
Austria	1,649	15
Denmark	1,644	22
Norway	1,627	24
France	1,481	27

Word work

Write five sentences about the survey using some of the phrases in the box.

> the survey has revealed
> which means that
> overall   the fewest
> more than … and … put together
> top, with over … is …
> more than fifty percent
> one in two   eight out of ten
> the vast majority
> … are among the …
> the average is …

Talk about it

Work in pairs. Discuss these questions.

- Are you surprised by these results?
- Is earning more money more important than taking a holiday from work? Why/Why not?
- How much annual holiday do you think workers should have?
- Do you remember family holidays when you were a child? What are your best memories of these times?
- Do you think your parents had enough holidays when you were younger?
- What other factors can make life stressful for today's workers?

Write about it

1 a Work in pairs. Discuss why commuting can cause a lot of stress for workers.

b Read the survey results and compare your ideas.

Commuting Survey

Number of commuters surveyed:	**2,955**
Average length of time spent commuting per year:	**139 hours**
Number of people consider commuting 'a waste of time':	**744**
Number of people enjoy reading while commuting:	**1,977**
Increase in people commuting over 50 km 1991-2007:	**30%**
Average length of commute before changing job:	**50 minutes**

Problems caused by car commuting:
high blood pressure, tension, bad moods, poor performance

Other effects:
less time for doctor's visits, sleep, exercise, eating healthily, leisure, social activities

2 Write a short report based on the survey results. Invent any additional information you think relevant. Use the phrases in the box to help you.

> **Useful language**
> This report is based on a survey of … and aims to show …
> Surprisingly/Unsurprisingly …
> People commented on…   It was found that …
> It comes as no surprise that …
> What concerned people was …
> What came out of the report quite clearly was that …

All change

Lead in

1 Work in pairs. Discuss these questions.

- How have you changed over the last five years (appearance, attitudes, personality, aims, etc.)?
- What events have changed you most in your life?
- What events in general can change people a lot?

2 Work with a different partner. Imagine you are meeting him/her five years into the future. Think about how your lives might change and then role play the conversation.

3 Tell the class how your partner has changed and what he/she has done in those five years.

Listen

1 🔊 21.1 Listen to the conversation. Who do the phrases refer to, Beth (B) or Gemma (G)?

1 is married

2 went to university

3 studied a lot at school

4 wanted to be an actor

5 has changed her appearance

2 🔊 21.1 Listen again. What significant events do Beth and Gemma mention that changed them?

3 Match the phrases 1–9 with phrases a–i.

1 You don't know, do you?	**a** I haven't looked back since.
2 I've had an operation on my nose.	**b** no ties
3 We stopped going out.	**c** I dropped out.
4 Got on with my life.	**d** You haven't got the faintest idea, have you?
5 no responsibilities	**e** You've got to move on.
6 You're not as …	**f** You're nowhere near as …
7 It was different to anything I'd expected.	**g** We split.
8 I have no regrets.	**h** I've had a nose job.
9 I left university before my course finished.	**i** It was a real shock to the system.

4 🔘 **21.1** **Work in pairs. Turn to page 90 and practise reading the dialogue. Try to stress the words in the same way as in the recording.**

Turn to page 90

Talk about it

1 **Work in pairs. Discuss the meanings of these expressions. Think of examples of situations where you might use them.**

1 A change is as good as a rest.

2 I'm stuck in a rut.

3 You can't teach an old dog new tricks.

4 It's a change for the better.

5 You need to turn your life around.

6 You shouldn't always play safe.

2 a **Choose one of the topics and prepare to talk for two minutes on how this can change people. Make notes and use the language in the box to help you.**

- starting work
- getting married
- retiring
- winning or inheriting a lot of money
- fame
- having a child

Useful language
a life changing event
it can make an enormous difference
things can never go back to how they were
it's a whole new way of life
you have to adapt to the new situation
your priorities suddenly change
there's no going back
no one can remain unchanged
it's like you're a different person

b **Work in small groups. Listen to each other's talks and discuss them. Do you agree with each other's ideas?**

Write about it

Write an e-mail to a friend telling him/her about a mutual friend you have just met after five years and talking about how they have changed.

Time on your side

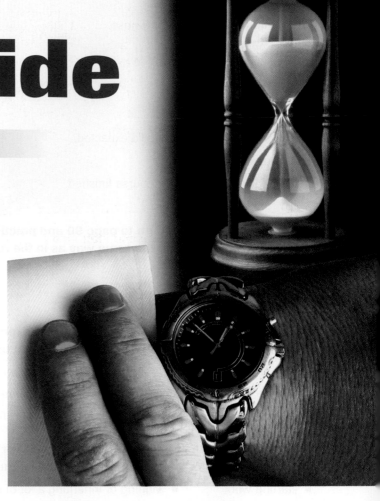

Lead in

1 Work in pairs. Discuss these questions.

- Are you a slave to time?
- Are you always punctual? When were you last late for something?
- Do you prioritise when you need to be punctual? How?
- Do you get irritated when things take longer than they should, e.g. meetings/traffic delays?
- Do you think you have good time management skills?
- Do you think people are becoming less punctual these days? Why?

2 Work in pairs. Read the comments about time. What do they mean? Do you agree with any of them? Why?

1 Punctuality is the thief of time.
Oscar Wilde

2 Punctuality is the virtue of the bored.
Evelyn Waugh

3 If I have made an appointment with you, I owe you punctuality, I have no right to throw away your time, if I do my own.
Richard Cecil

4 Punctuality is the soul of business.
Thomas Chandler Haliburton

Word work

1 Work in pairs. Discuss the meaning of the expressions in the box. Can you add any more with the word *time*?

time after time	time-saving
on time	time limit
in time	from time to time
time on your side	out of time
small time/big time	kill time
the time of your life	on borrowed time
it's high time	timely

2 Rewrite the sentences using expressions from Exercise 1.

1 I've told you again and again to back up your work on the computer.

2 I don't think she'll stay in this job for long since she had that argument with the boss.

3 You only have an hour to finish this work.

4 We had an absolutely amazing day out in London.

5 I'm sorry, you have to finish now.

Listen

1 🔘 `22.1` **Listen to Jackie's anecdote and answer the questions.**

    1 Is the language formal or informal?

    2 What do you think would be the best title for the story? Why?

       An excellent journey   *What a success!*
       Happy times   *Home at last*

2 🔘 `22.1` **Listen again and choose the correct answer, a or b.**

    1 The speaker was:
       a on holiday.   **b** on a course.

    2 The speaker was concerned about:
       a getting home.   **b** getting a meal.

    3 The presentation:
       a finished on time.   **b** overran.

    4 The meal was paid for by:
       a the company.   **b** the speaker.

    5 The speaker:
       a only had to wait for one train.
       b didn't have to wait for any trains.

3 **Work in pairs. Think of more formal language to replace the <u>underlined</u> words.**

    1 <u>By rights</u> the day should've been a disaster.

    2 I knew getting back to Southampton on the train that evening was going to be <u>pretty tight</u>.

    3 Anyway, <u>I did my bit</u> and <u>no kidding</u> – as soon as I finished my last word, the buzzer sounded!

    4 So, Pete and I <u>hot footed it</u> to the station with no idea of train times.

    5 We <u>hopped on</u> and ten seconds later it left. <u>How jammy was that</u>?

    6 By then we were <u>starving</u>.

    7 I <u>figured</u> I'd probably have to wake up some friend in London and <u>kip</u> on their floor.

    8 If I could <u>make it</u> across London in fifteen minutes <u>I stood an outside chance</u> of catching the last train from Waterloo.

    9 I <u>legged it</u> to the tube station.

    10 <u>Thinking back</u> if I'd been a couple of seconds later at any point in the day it wouldn't have worked.

4 **Work in pairs. Write three gapped sentences using the phrases in Exercise 3. Swap your sentences with your partner and complete them.**

Talk about it

Prepare to tell an anecdote about one of these subjects or one of your own. Use the phrases in the box to help you.

- a day when everything went right/wrong
- an amazing coincidence
- a lucky event

> **Useful language**
> it was …   then …   just as …
>   as soon as …   after …
> in the end …   it turned out …

Write about it

A magazine is inviting readers to write an anecdote for a competition. Write your entry.

Happiness

Lead in

1 Work in pairs. Discuss these questions.

- What does *happiness* mean to you?
- Should we actively search for happiness or does it come on its own?
- Has the idea of happiness changed over the generations?
- Do you think people in general are happier today than they were in the past?

Word work

1 a Work in pairs. Take a piece of paper and write down as many words as you can to do with being happy or sad.

b Look at the words in the box. Did you write any of these?

> happy   contented   blissful   overjoyed   ecstatic   delirious
> elated   sad   depressed   miserable   fed up   down   suicidal

2 Which adjectives in Exercise 1 do you think describe normal feelings? Which do you think are extreme?

Read about it

1 a Work in pairs. Read the question and compare your ideas.

> **What do you think contributes to people's unhappiness today?**

b On a website people mentioned the topics in the box. How do you think they are connected to unhappiness? Discuss your ideas with the class.

> the media   materialism
> close communities   families
> poverty   television
> advertising   selfishness
> unfairness in society

2 a Work in pairs. Think of suggestions to address the problems in Exercise 1.

b Scan the comments A–E posted on a website and match them with the topics in Exercise 1. There are more topics than comments.

A I see news programmes as a contributor to unhappiness in the UK. They only report sensationalist bad news and make people feel angry and depressed. We never hear about the really good things that are going on in the world.

B I believe that materialism and consumerism serve to make people unhappy. The media is to blame for this. Through advertising we are constantly being told that we need more of this and should have more of that and they hold up models of perfect families which we compare ourselves against and feel inferior. This just breeds discontent. And having money and all the possessions we can buy doesn't bring us happiness. That comes from inside.

C The days of close family and community spirit seem to be fast vanishing. Even in the 1990s there was more social cohesion. This is not just in cities but in towns and even villages. In my village some people don't even know their neighbours properly. Therefore the slightest thing can cause arguments, like loud music and rowdy behaviour. If people knew each other things would be resolved much more peacefully.

D Promote and ensure fairness in all things in society. When people witness vast gaps in wages, wealth, health and opportunity then this breeds discontentment. With the explosion of television media coverage, people can now see first hand the clear divide between the haves and the have nots.

E Severe restrictions, if not an outright ban, on television should definitely be the first and most important step. Families sit gormlessly in front of the television failing to communicate at all. Instead of going out to parties, making friends, or having people round for dinner, people just sit and gawp at that little black box in the corner of the room. Children watch soaps and dramas where some amazing life changing events happen every day. They grow up thinking that's how life should be. And it isn't.

3 **Read the comments again. Which ones include references to these things?**

1 television _____
2 advertising _____
3 the news _____
4 neighbours _____
5 socialising _____
6 wages _____

4 **Find words or phrases in the comments with these meanings.**

1 attention grabbing _____
2 disappearing _____
3 causes unhappiness _____
4 encourage _____
5 complete _____
6 stare _____
7 for themselves _____

Talk about it

Work in pairs and discuss these questions.

- Which of website comments, if any, do you agree with? Why?
- Which of them do you disagree with? Why?
- Do you think the survey findings reflect the majority view or not?

Write about it

Write your own comment to post on the website.

File in bin

Lead in

Work in pairs. Discuss these questions.

- What is *junk mail*? What is the meaning of *junk* and what else can it be used to describe?

- What does junk mail include?

- How do you feel about getting junk mail?

- What do you do with it?

- What problems can it cause?

- How else do we receive unwanted advertising?

Read about it

1 Read the first part of a newspaper article and decide if the statements are true (T) or false (F).

1 The Royal Mail sent out a leaflet to help their customers.

2 The Royal Mail makes money from delivering junk mail.

3 Roger Annies wanted to help The Royal Mail.

2 Work in pairs. Discuss the questions.

1 Do you think the postman was right to do what he did? Why/Why not?

2 What do you think the rest of the article might be about?

Roger Annies, a postman, recently found himself in trouble with his employer The Royal Mail. He delivered a leaflet, which he had written himself, informing all the households on his round how to avoid receiving junk mail. The Royal Mail, which makes a significant profit from distributing this type of mail, was understandably unhappy with Mr Annies' actions and his job is now in the balance.

This story has served to highlight an increasing problem …

3 a Match words from 1–10 with words from a–j to make expressions and collocations.

1	mail discarded	**a**	of the problem
2	unsolicited	**b**	simple steps
3	cold	**c**	correspondence
4	scale	**d**	impact
5	a rash of	**e**	unopened
6	accounts for	**f**	out
7	environmental	**g**	enquiries
8	opt	**h**	calling
9	not in	**i**	a third of all post
10	take	**j**	the interest of

b Work in pairs. Compare your answers and discuss possible contexts for them in the remainder of the newspaper article.

Write about it

1 a Work in pairs. Look at the information taken from the complete newspaper article and discuss the meaning of the words in *italics*.

1 21 billion pieces of junk mail are sent each year.

2 550,000 tonnes of direct mail were posted last year.

3 Green *campaigners* are worried about environment.

4 Customers can contact *Mail Preference Service*.

5 Since 1997 there has been an increase in junk mail of 65%.

6 Each *household* receives approximately 18 items a week.

7 Junk mail *makes up* 4% of waste paper in UK.

8 The Government spent more than £1 million on direct mail in 2004.

9 In some places in Europe *distributors* limit delivery days.

10 *Spam* makes up one third of all email traffic.

11 Laws targeting spam have many *loopholes*.

12 The whole area of junk mail needs government *regulation*.

b Divide the information into three categories: Amount, Environment and Solutions.

2 Write the rest of the article using some of the information from Exercise 1 and adding any other information you may know.

Use the beginning of the article on page 50 as your introductory paragraph.

Plan what information will go in each paragraph.

- introduction
- first issue
- second issue
- possible action
- conclusion

3 Work in pairs. You have been asked to write an article on the same subject for a teenage magazine. Discuss how this would be different from the newspaper article and then write the piece for the magazine.

How are **you?**

Lead in

Work in pairs. Discuss these questions.

- Do you think people are healthier these days than they used to be?
- What do you do to keep yourself fit and healthy?
- What do you know about the health system in the UK?

Read about it

1 Read about the health system in the UK. Are there any facts that surprise you?

In the UK there are two types of health care: the NHS, which is funded from taxes, and private health care organisations, which people pay into directly. Treatment on the NHS is free but because of queues to see specialists and long delays in treatment, many of the people who can afford to 'go private'. They are guaranteed immediate or relatively quick treatment in comfortable surroundings. The NHS has a limited amount of money to spend and has to balance its books. It is therefore very aware of where its money goes. This has lead to prioritisation of certain procedures and lack of availability of some potentially life-saving drugs because of the expense involved. There are currently many debates going on over which types of treatment should receive funding. The issues involved are very controversial and the decisions that the NHS makes are difficult and often extremely unpopular.

2 Work in pairs. Compare the health system in the UK with the health system in your country.

Talk about it

1 Look at the headlines about recent health issues. What do you think the stories are about?

2 Work in pairs and compare your ideas about the headlines in Exercise 1. Are there similar issues with funding, procedures and drugs in your country?

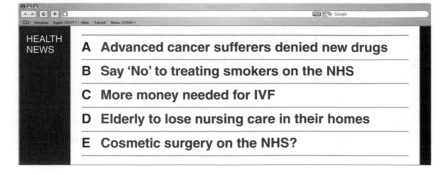

HEALTH NEWS

A Advanced cancer sufferers denied new drugs

B Say 'No' to treating smokers on the NHS

C More money needed for IVF

D Elderly to lose nursing care in their homes

E Cosmetic surgery on the NHS?

Listen

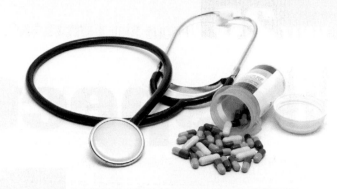

1 **[25.1]** **Listen and complete the dialogues with the words in the box**

pushed	priority	damaging	stopped	single
up to	pricy	care	miracle cure	nose job

1

A: (1) _____ women are going to be given treatment on the NHS. How good is that?

B: I'm not so sure. Couples should get (2) _____, surely.

2

A: Apparently, you get (3) _____ right down the transplant lists for hearts and livers. That's so unfair.

B: Is it? You can understand it, though. I mean, if you don't take (4) _____ of yourself …

3

A: I think it's appalling! It's a (5) _____ and they say it's too (6) _____ to give people. I mean, what is research all about?

B: But it only gives an extra six months of life.

4

A: Did you know that you can get a (7) _____ on the NHS now?

B: That's only if the size is (8) _____ you psychologically!

5

A: The cutbacks are really affecting my gran. All sorts of care services are being (9) _____.

B: Yes. But surely it's (10) _____ the family to help out.

2 Match the conversations 1–5 with the headlines A–E on page 52.

Talk about it

1 **a** Read the expressions in the box and <u>underline</u> where you think the stress should be.

1 It's scandalous that people should have to …

2 It's completely unethical to …

3 We have to be realistic.

4 You can't expect to …

5 Can you honestly say that …

6 Are you saying that …?

7 I'm sorry, I don't understand what you're trying to say.

8 This is something I feel particularly strongly about.

b **[25.2]** Listen and check.

2 Work in pairs. Choose one of the headlines on page 52 and make notes about why the cause deserves more money. Prepare to give your opinions to the class. Make a note of why some people might be against the other causes receiving a lot of money.

3 Present your cause to the class. Discuss the issues involved with the rest of the class.

Write about it

Choose one of the headlines and write the article for it.

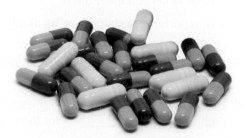

Respect

Lead in

Work in pairs. Discuss these questions.

- Name a person from these categories who you respect a lot and say why.
  1 a famous person
  2 a friend or colleague
  3 a family member
  4 a certain profession

- Do you think older people or those in authority automatically deserve respect or do they need to earn it?

- Some people say that manners are a 'social lubricant'. What do you think this means and do you agree?

Word work

Do you understand the differences between the pairs of words in the box? Complete the sentences then check your answers in a dictionary.

> respect/admiration   custom/tradition
> manners/etiquette   respectable/respectful
> consideration/concern

1 People should always have _____ for their parents whatever they have done.

2 It's a long held _____ in our family that we open our Christmas presents after the evening meal.

3 In many countries it is the _____ to kiss friends when you meet them.

4 It is important for children to be taught good _____ from an early age.

5 In the past, living with a partner without being married was not considered _____.

6 People who have parties out in the garden late at night have no _____ for their neighbours.

Listen

1 a **You are going to hear members of a family (mother, father, older daughter and younger son) talking about respect and manners. What differences do you think there will be between the speakers?**

b 🔘 `26.1` **Listen and check if you were right.**

2 🔘 `26.1` **Listen again. Who do the phrases refer to, the mother (M), father (F), daughter (D) or son (S)?**

1 thinks parents should respect their children

2 thinks some young people are respectful

3 thinks respect doesn't depend on age

4 used to be religious

5 was taught to respect older people early on

6 suggests a way of helping to improve behaviour

7 thinks respect depends on how we treat other people

8 thinks people used to respect others who didn't necessarily deserve it

3 a Work in pairs. Complete the sentences with the correct word, a, b or c.

1 There are by- _____ of religion when it comes to respect.
   a reasons   **b** products   **c** remains

2 If they had a _____ where they could talk about what respect is all about, it might improve their behaviour.
   a formation   **b** foreign place   **c** forum

3 There was a(n) _____ in previous generations that certain people commanded respect and they didn't have to earn it.
   a assumption   **b** resumption   **c** consumption

4 There's more of a _____ now and people feel you need to earn respect.
   a aristocracy   **b** autocracy   **c** meritocracy

5 People of different _____ get respected differently.
   a state   **b** estate   **c** status

6 Some people don't give as much respect as they should to their_____.
   a olders   **b** elders   **c** others

b 🔘 **26.2** Listen to check your answers. Check the meanings of any words you don't understand in the dictionary.

Talk about it

1 a Work in pairs. Look at the list of actions which some people might find offensive. Answer the questions. Look at the phrases in the box to help you.

- Are these examples of bad manners?
- Is this behaviour considered bad manners in your country?

> **Useful language**
> In my opinion it's …   You should never …   That is *so* rude!
> People in my country would never …   No, that's accepted.
> It's considered very bad manners to …

1 swearing in public.

2 blowing your nose in public

3 queue jumping

4 not being punctual

5 eating with your mouth open

6 not apologising if you bump into someone.

7 eating from your knife

8 burping loudly in public

9 not putting your knife and fork together on the plate when you have finished

10 staring at other people

11 asking how much someone earns

12 spitting in the street

13 yawning or coughing with your mouth uncovered

14 using bread to wipe your plate in a restaurant

15 talking with a mouthful of food

16 slurping your drink

17 taking your shoes off in a public place

2 Compare your ratings with other students. Write another list of things that are considered bad manners in your country. Discuss them in class.

Write about it

Write a short paragraph describing your attitude to respect to read out in a class forum.

Reader,
I married him

Lead in

Work in pairs. Discuss these questions.

- What are you reading at the moment?
- Do you prefer reading newspapers, magazines or novels?
- When do you usually read?
- Do you read a lot in English?
- What was the first book you read in English? Did you enjoy it? Why/Why not?
- Do you know the names of any English writers?

Read about it

1 Work in pairs, Student A and Student B.

Student A: read Extract A.
Student B: read Extract B.

Ask and answer the questions. Make a note of your partner's answers.

1 What is the name of the narrator?

2 What type of book is it?

3 Who else is mentioned in the extract?

4 What do we learn about the narrator?

5 How is the narrator feeling?

6 What happens or has happened?

7 Find at least five adjectives from your extract.

2 Look at the answers you have noted down. How different are the two books? Are there any similarities?

3 Look at the lists of adjectives you selected in Exercise 1. What do you think they tell you about the different writers and the stories?

4 Read your partner's extract. Which do you prefer and why?

Write about it

1 Work in pairs. Choose one of the extracts on page 57 and discuss what you think happens on the next page. Note down your ideas.

2 Write the second page of the book. Think about: events. style and vocabulary.

❧ ❧ A ❧ ❧

A lot of people hated Marshal Bede. They hated him with a real, passionate hatred. Not the hatred you feel fleetingly for someone who's nicked the parking space you've been waiting for. Nor the hatred you feel, which is more like envy, for someone who's so beautiful or good-looking you want to cut their hair off or force feed them chocolate for days on end. Not even the hatred you feel for a previously good friend who's going out with the guy or girl you fancied at the party. No, Marshal Bede was hated with the hatred which makes you want to kill. I should know. I was one of those people. I once set my students an exercise to find suitably nasty adjectives beginning with every letter of the alphabet so that I could revile him comprehensively in the safety of my own brain. So I wasn't surprised when he was found dead one Tuesday morning. The only surprise was that it wasn't me who killed him.

So, who am I? Well, let me introduce myself. My name is Alex Gray and I'm a teacher as you may have guessed. Marshal Bede was my boss – the principal of a prosperous, thriving boarding school for the teenage children of parents with more money than sense. Mind you, considering the general behaviour of the delightful little brats, perhaps their parents do have some sense after all.

But back to the boss. Marshal was a very nasty little man. Red in the face through an over fondness of red wine and whisky (not necessarily together, although I wouldn't have put it past him) and short and pompous. Like many vertically challenged people before him, he felt the need to preside over the school with total domination and dictatorship which humbled all those so much in need of a job that they would nod wisely at his rantings to his face and berate him in the safety of the loos and the staffroom. I was one of these. Some might call me a coward. I prefer 'rational' and 'security conscious'. As for the adjectives that my students intelligently produced, we could start with aggressive, belligerent, cocky, dictatorial, egocentric … But I don't want to get too vindictive. At least, not yet.

★ ★ B ★ ★

The first time Nina heard the voice was in the queue for check-in. It was a distinctive voice – low, mellow and one she could imagine sending shivers down phone lines across the world. It certainly set the hairs on the back of her neck tingling.

It was a simple statement, nothing dramatically sexy. 'I didn't expect the queue to be this long so early,' the voice murmured. She agreed wholeheartedly as she viewed the line of people winding their way around the poles connected with blue tape. But there was something about the voice that unnerved her. It carried down the queue without being loud, resonating with a barely concealed sexual energy.

Nina flicked a few strands of damp hair from her eyes and glanced very casually backward to see if the face fitted the voice. Unfortunately, the speaker was several people behind her in the queue and turned away from her so that she could only see his back. What was clear was that he was accompanied by an extremely attractive tall blonde with her hair tumbling onto her slim shoulders. Nina wondered idly how much time and money it had taken for the result to look so casual and then admonished herself for being so catty. The blonde held a protective arm around the man's shoulders and as Nina watched he touched his lips to the nape of her neck.

What she could see of the speaker sharpened Nina's interest. The man was tall and dark, wearing a light linen suit and he stood straight, with the confidence of someone who knows he's attractive. However, to Nina's annoyance, at the moment he started to turn back the passenger behind her shuffled with her suitcases into just the wrong position.

'Oh well,' sighed Nina, 'I'll just have to use my imagination' – an activity she had been indulging in quite a lot recently. She gave her suitcase a hefty shove forward with her foot. A few inches closer.

What bugs **you?**

Lead in

1 Complete this questionnaire. Mark your answers 1–5 (1 = very/often, 5 = not at all/never). Discuss your answers with another student.

1 How patient are you?

2 How often do you have a good rant?

3 How often do you complain orally if you're unhappy with a situation?

4 How often do you complain in writing?

5 Do these things annoy you? How much? What would you do in these situations?

A Your neighbours make a lot of noise at night with their motorbikes.

B You have waited a long time to be served in a restaurant.

C The meal you receive in a restaurant is below standard.

D Non-essential road works are carried out in the rush hour on a busy motorway.

E Your train is regularly late.

F Non-essential road works are carried out in the rush hour on a busy motorway.

G You want to cancel a phone contract but you are left on hold for more than half an hour.

H Another driver takes a parking space you have been waiting for.

2 Work in pairs. Think of five more situations that annoy you.

3 Work with another partner. Compare the situations you listed in Exercise 2. Give examples of situations like these you have been in and how you reacted. You can use some of the expressions in the box in your conversation.

> **Useful language**
> I know exactly what you mean!
> That is *so* annoying!
> I get particularly angry when …
> No, that doesn't really bother me. It's when …
> That really bugs me!
> That is such a pain!   Tell me about it!

Word work

Look at the expressions in the box. Is the speaker reacting (R) or not reacting (N)?

1 I really let rip

2 it gets my back up

3 I let it wash over me

4 it's not worth the hassle

5 I don't like to make a fuss

6 I don't like to take things lying down

7 life's too short

8 anything for a quiet life

9 you can't let people walk all over you

10 you can always find something to moan about

1 🔘 **28.1** Without looking at the recording script below, listen to someone talking about a situation she is not happy with. Note down the points she is complaining about.

2 🔘 **28.1** Listen again and <u>underline</u> words that are stressed. Listen again and repeat, paying attention to stress patterns.

> I'm going to have a good rant here. I cannot understand why they don't put extra trains on at the height of the rush hour. It's appalling. We pay sky-high prices to travel by train every day and then we're forced to stand for the whole journey, elbow to elbow with other poor commuters. The carriages are so packed they get really smelly and there's no way you can get to the buffet for a coffee – mind you, there'd be no way you could drink the coffee standing up without spilling it all over yourself and other passengers! Not the safest way to travel! By the time I get to work in the mornings, my back aches, my feet hurt, my clothes are creased and smelly and I'm so frazzled it takes ages to unwind.

3 Read the same person's letter to the rail company. Look at the highlighted words. Which more informal words did she use when she was speaking?

Dear Sir/Madam

I commute daily to London on your 7.30 train from Westchester and I am writing to tell you how disappointed I am in the service.

The train is regularly overcrowded, forcing people to stand in the aisles for the duration of the journey. Not only is this uncomfortable, but it is also, in my considered opinion, breaching health and safety regulations.

The fares we pay to travel in such poor conditions are exorbitant and I request a refund of an appropriate percentage of my season ticket. I also demand that you supply additional carriages to deal with the increased number of passengers travelling at peak times.

I await your reply,

Yours,

1 🔘 **28.2** Listen to someone talking about a different situation and make notes of the points mentioned.

2 Write a letter of complaint to the holiday company using the points mentioned by the speaker.

Green light

Lead in

Work in pairs. Discuss these questions.

- Some people say that global warming is not happening and that the environmental crisis has been exaggerated. Why do you think they say this? What do you think?

- In what ways do you think you damage the environment?

- Do you do anything to help the environment?

Word work

Match the expressions with two groups of people: 1 those who believe global warming is happening and 2 those who don't believe global warming is happening.

a **They've got their heads in the sand.**

b **It's all scare tactics.**

c **They're just delaying the inevitable.**

d **They're just jumping to conclusions.**

e **They're walking around blindfold.**

f **They've got another agenda.**

g **The evidence is all contradictory.**

Listen

1 🔘 **29.1** **Listen to a presentation and answer the questions.**

1 What is the purpose of the speech?

2 What is the problem he outlines?

3 What examples of solutions does he give?

2 **Look at the recording script on page 93 and <u>underline</u> phrases that show that this is a speech.**

3 a Work in pairs. Look at the expressions for giving a presentation. Think of ways of completing them.

1 The first point I'd like to make is …

2 I'm in the lucky position of being able to …

3 I'll try to be as brief as I can.

4 Everyone knows that …

5 If you look at the handout, you'll see that …

6 Following on from that …

7 Let's move on.

8 I'd like to finish by saying …

9 It's been a real pleasure …

b 🔘 **29.2** Listen and repeat. Pay attention to the intonation.

Talk about it

1 Work in small groups. Discuss these questions.

- How do supermarkets contribute to environmental problems?
- How do airline companies contribute to environmental problems?
- How can schools best help educate children about environmental problems?

2 Work in groups of three. Choose a role, A, B or C, and follow the steps to prepare a presentation.

1 Discuss what steps can be taken to help the environment by the relevant people involved.

2 Individually, use ideas from this discussion to prepare to give a two-minute presentation for your role.

3 Read the presentation text again to remind yourselves of useful language.

Role A

You are the representative of a major supermarket. You are going to talk at a conference on the environment. You should talk about what the supermarket already does in its 'Go Green' campaign and also plans for future improvements.

Role B

You are the owner of a big airline and you are going to give a talk to the press about your plans to donate money to the 'Green Cause' and also to lower carbon emissions to help the environment.

Role C

You are the head teacher at a primary school and you are going to give a talk to parents and governors about how you plan to increase children's awareness of environmental problems at your school over the coming years.

3 Form different groups of three.

1 Give your presentation to the group.

2 Discuss the different points made in the talks and decide which ideas you think are realistic and useful.

Write about it

Write a short report on either your own or another student's speech for *Green Light Magazine*. Try to use some of the reporting verbs in the box in your report.

started	added	insisted	explained	hoped	warned	finished

Memories are **made of this**

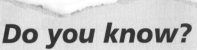

Lead in

1 Listen to a list of objects. Try to remember as many as you can. Do not write them down.

2 Do the quiz and compare your answers with another student.

Do you know?

1 How many items in a list can the average person remember?

2 Why can 'forgetting things' sometimes be a good thing?

3 Why do smells bring back vivid memories?

4 What is the average age for the earliest memories?

5 Which foods can boost brain power and improve the memory?

6 Does memory improve the more you use it?

7 After what age can we generally remember more autobiographical details?

8 How many people report a 'déjà vu' experience?

9 What is a 'flashbulb' memory?

3 Write down as many items from the list in Exercise 1 that you memorised. How many did you remember?

4 Listen to your teacher's instructions. Were you able to do the task correctly? What does this tell us about memory?

Word work

Complete the table with appropriate words.

verb	noun	adjective
remember		
forget		
recall		
remind		
reminisce		
memorise		
	nostalgia	

Listen

1 🔊 **30.1** Listen to people talking about aspects of memory and match the speakers 1–4 to the topics a–d.

a forgetting **b** earliest memory **c** déjà vu **d** false memory

2 🔊 **30.1** Listen again and draw a picture of what Tom could see.

3 🔊 **30.1** Listen again. Why are these items important in the accounts?

1 a rabbit **2** a tree **3** a tennis game **4** black smoke

Talk about it

1 Work in pairs. Tell each other about these things.

- your earliest memory
- a time you forgot something important
- any strange premonitions or déjà vu experiences you have had
- a memory you are not sure is real or not

2 Work in pairs. Discuss these questions.

1 What is your memory like?

2 Do you have any techniques to help you remember things?

3 Match the techniques in the box with the examples 1–8.

> chunking   cramming   external aids   place it   routine
> word play   make it meaningful   imagery

1 I always write things down in my diary.

2 I break things like long numbers down into easier bits.

3 I always leave my keys in the same place.

4 I remember the first letters of the things I have to remember.

5 I remember lists by imagining the things in different places in my house.

6 Before exams I try to remember lots of things in a really short time.

7 With long numbers I try to relate them to things that mean something to me – like birthdays, famous dates in history, etc.

8 I remember lists and things by linking them to bizarre pictures!

4 a Write down these things.

- a number with nine digits.
- a list of ten items for a shopping list.
- ten things you might take on holiday with you

b Work in pairs. Test each other's memory using these lists. Try to use the 'place it' technique to remember one list, 'imagery' to remember another and 'chunking' to remember the numbers. Did any of them work?

Junk **culture**

Lead in

Work in pairs. Discuss these questions.

- What do you think *junk culture* is?
- Do you think children's lives today are better or worse than they were when you/your parents were young?

Read about it

1 a You are going to read an article from *The Daily Telegraph* about the effect of junk culture on today's children. What topics do you think it will mention?

b Read the article and check your answers.

Junk culture 'is poisoning our children'

A sinister cocktail of junk food, marketing, over-competitive schooling and electronic entertainment is poisoning childhood according to a powerful lobby of academics and children's experts. In a letter to this newspaper they call on the Government to act to prevent the death of childhood.

They write: 'We are deeply concerned at the escalating incidence of childhood depression and children's behavioural and developmental conditions.' The group blames a failure by politicians and public alike to understand how children develop. 'Since children's brains are still developing, they cannot adjust … to the effects of ever more rapid technological and cultural change,' they write. 'They still need what developing human beings have always needed, including real food (as opposed to 'junk'), real play (as opposed to sedentary, screen-based entertainment), first-hand experience of the world they live in and regular interaction with real-life significant adults in their lives.

They also need time. In a fast-moving, hyper-competitive culture, today's children are expected to cope with an ever-earlier start to formal schoolwork and an overly academic test-driven primary curriculum.

They are pushed by market forces to act and dress like mini-adults and exposed via the electronic media to material which would have been considered unsuitable for children even in the recent past.'

Sue Palmer, a former head teacher and author of *Toxic Childhood* said: 'Children's development is being drastically affected by the kind of world they are brought up in. A child's physical and psychological growth cannot be accelerated. It changes in biological time, not at electrical speed. Childhood is not a race.'

2 Tick the points in the box that are mentioned in the article. Make a note of the context for each topic.

> depression   technological change   food   computer games
> time   competition   tests   fashion   music   unsuitable material
> debate   tattoos and piercings   bullying   exercise

3 Find words in the article on page 64 with these meanings.

1 evil _____
2 rising quickly _____
3 worried _____
4 very fast _____
5 seated _____
6 important _____
7 excessively _____
8 deal with _____
9 shown _____
10 poisonous _____

4 a Complete the compound adjectives from the article.

1 _____-hand
2 _____-life
3 _____-moving
4 _____-competitive
5 _____-earlier
6 _____-driven

b Write five gapped sentences using some of the compounds. Work in pairs and complete each other's sentences.

Talk about it

Work in pairs. Discuss these questions.

- Does the situation described in the letter exist in your country?
- Do you agree with the reasons given for children's mental problems today? Why/Why not?
- Are there any other factors not mentioned in the article that you think cause depression in today's children?
- Do you think today's parents are 'worse' than they used to be? Why/Why not?
- Do you think that people can be taught how to be 'good' parents?
- What part should governments play in protecting children's childhood?
- Some people say that we can't turn back the clock. We have to accept that life is going to be different for our children. What do you think?

Write about it

Write a Letter to the Editor giving your reaction to the article on page 64. Include these points.

- what you agree/disagree with in the article and your reasons
- possible action that could be taken

Talk to me

Lead in

1 Work in pairs. Do the quiz and discuss your answers.

Quick Quiz

1 Where is your mobile phone now?

2 Is it switched on or off? Why/Why not?

3 Do you usually keep your phone switched on all the time?

4 How old were you when you had your first mobile phone?

5 How many phones have you had? Can you remember the makes?

6 What do you usually use your phone for?

7 If you lost your phone, would you lose any really important information?

2 Work in pairs. Discuss these questions.

- Why do mobile phones continue to increase in popularity?

- Are there any occasions when writing an email or letter would be better than making a call?

- Are there any times or places where you should switch off your phone?

Read about it

1 a Work in pairs. Read the titles of each text on page 67. Discuss the points which might be included in the texts.

b Read the texts quickly and check whether your ideas are included or not.

2 a Read the texts again. Do you agree with what they say? Why/Why not? Which of the points in the box are not included?

> mobility   sending messages
> using a camera   being talkative
> safety   companionship
> changing plans   using the Internet

b Find phrases or sentences that refer to the other points in the box.

Word work

1 Complete the phrases 1–8 with words in the box.

> across   in   about   in   up   on   in   out of   out

1 keep _____ touch

2 _____ the move

3 meet _____

4 come _____ your shell

5 day _____ day _____

6 keep tabs _____

7 come _____

8 talking _____

a on the subject of

b stay in contact

c all the time

d give the right impression

e stop being shy

f while travelling

g get together

h know someone's movements

2 Match the phrases 1–8 with the meanings a–h. Check your answers in the texts on page 67.

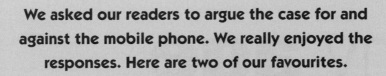 

We asked our readers to argue the case for and against the mobile phone. We really enjoyed the responses. Here are two of our favourites.

Switch me on!

Switch me on and I open life up for you. With me in your pocket you have the freedom to go wherever you like but still keep in touch. You can organise your day on the move. Like changing that date: 'Let's go to that new restaurant instead. And can we make it 7.30 not 7.00?' Like changing your mind: 'Sorry, really too tired to meet up tonight. How about tomorrow … or next week … or next year!' Switch me on and you can stop people worrying: 'Sorry, stuck at the office in a bus/in traffic/in the supermarket queue.' (Zara's really, but what's a porky here or there between friends?) And I get you interacting with people, coming out of your shell a bit. It's good to talk, to text, to send photos and videos … to share. But what I'm really good at is making you feel safe and secure. I can be with you day in day out and I'm always there when you need me. Just keep me switched on …

Switch off that phone!

Give everyone a break! And give yourself a break too. Think how good it can be for you to be 'unavailable' from time to time. You can do whatever you want without the inevitable interruptions from your pocket or bag. Switch it off and no one can keep tabs on you. Remember what that freedom used to be like? With it switched off you can also give a face to face conversation the attention it deserves. It says you care more about the person you're with than whoever might be on the other end of that little machine that is manically ringing in your pocket. And talking about face to face, it's sometimes good to give people the gift of your time and attention, especially to talk about things that don't come across so well text to text or voice to voice! We all know that we couldn't live without our phones – but just occasionally it's fun to try asserting control and switching off for a while. Could you?

Write about it

1 **Work in pairs. Think of points for and against these things.**

- taking holidays abroad/taking holidays in your own country
- going straight to university after school/ taking a gap year before university
- commuting by train/commuting by car

2 **Choose one of the topics in Exercise 1 and write two short articles for the magazine giving opposing viewpoints. Use the language in the box to help you. Start your articles with an interesting statement or question to catch the reader's attention.**

> **Useful language**
> A point of view in favour of … is
> One reason you should/shouldn't … is …
> An obvious advantage of … is …
> It is said that …
> We mustn't forget that …
> Another important point to consider is …

It's my **age**

Lead in

Work in pairs. Discuss these questions.

- Do you enjoy being the age you are? What are the advantages and disadvantages?
- What has been the best age for you so far? Why?
- Have you ever had any problems because of your age – being too young or too old?

Word work

1 Look at the photos. Which of the words in the box do you associate with them?

> juvenile
> life expectancy
> precocious   discrimination
> wisdom   maturity
> ageism

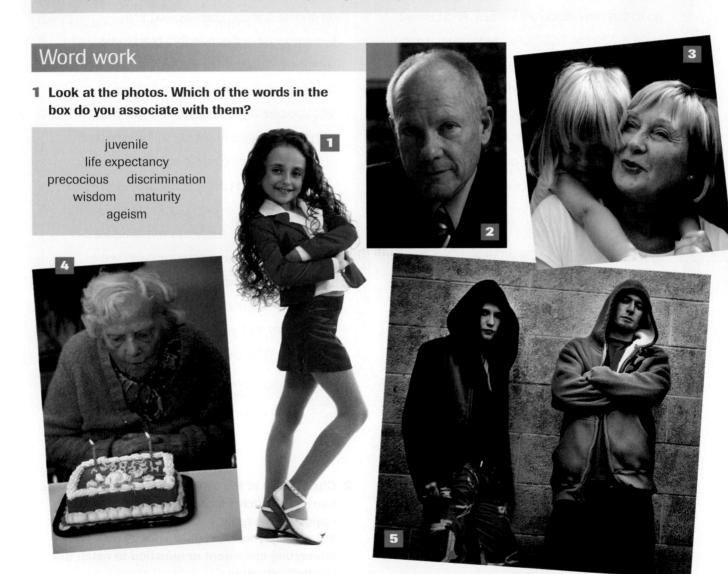

2 How many different words can you make from the roots of the words in Exercise 1? Which word is both an adjective and a noun? Check your answers in a dictionary.

3 Complete the sentences with the correct form of one of the words in Exercise 1.

1 It is illegal to _____ against women in the workforce.

2 Some employers have very _____ attitudes towards older workers.

3 He's seventeen but he's very _____.

4 Most people can _____ to live beyond seventy-five nowadays.

Read about it

1 **Read the article and decide which picture on page 68 it is related to.**

A new employment law introduced in October 2006 has meant the biggest shake up in anti-discrimination law for over twenty-five years in the UK. It is now illegal to discriminate against a worker under the age of sixty-five on the grounds of age. In practice this means that age should not affect recruitment, training or promotion, and this applies to the young as well as the older worker. It will also mean that employers can no longer force employees to retire early. Certain industries, including those where physical strength is a priority, will be exempt from the law. However, many employers are concerned that the UK will see a surge in the number of unfair dismissal cases brought, as has happened in Ireland since a similar law came into force there. Indeed, in the USA it is reported that that there are currently more cases brought concerning age discrimination than sex or race. In spite of the new law it is thought that it will take a long time for employers to change their ingrained attitudes to older workers

2 **Complete the expressions with words from the article.**

1 unfair _____

2 a shake-_____

3 come into _____

4 a _____ in the number of

5 on the _____ of

6 ingrained _____

7 to be exempt _____

3 **Write three gapped sentences with some of the collocations in Exercise 2. Work in pairs and complete each other's sentences.**

Listen

1 🔘 **33.1** **Listen to the dialogue and decide which photo on page 68 it is related to.**

2 a **Try to remember words from the dialogue with these meanings.**

1 stop having

2 stay longer than necessary

3 active

4 mental abilities

b 🔘 **33.1** **Listen again to check.**

Talk about it

Work in pairs. Look at the pictures on page 68 and talk about the different aspects of age that they show. Use the questions for your discussion.

1 Would you encourage a young child to pursue a talent? Why/Why not?

2 What can a grandchild and grandparent give each other?

3 Would you give up anything to live to one hundred? Why/Why not?

4 Do you think it's right for employers to be penalised for hiring and firing workers of a particular age? Why/Why not?

5 Should juvenile offenders be treated in the same way as older offenders? Why/Why not?

Write about it

Choose picture 1, 4 or 5 and write a short article for a magazine based on the points you have discussed.

What's the **catch?**

Lead in

Work in pairs. Discuss these questions.

- What is a *scam*? Check in your dictionary.
- Have you ever been the victim of a scam? Do you know anyone who has?
- Do you know of any famous scams?
- How can people avoid being the victim of a scam?

Word work

1 a Do you understand the differences in meaning of the words in the box? Check your ideas in a dictionary.

> scam   con   trick   hoax   fraud   practical joke

b Answer the questions.

1 Find words from the box to complete the nouns for the people who do these things.
   a _____ artist   **b** _____ster   **c** _____er

2 Which of the words are verbs as well as nouns?

3 Which words collocate with these verbs?
   a play _____   **b** commit _____   **c** run _____

4 What are the adjectival forms of these words?
   a fraud _____   **b** trick _____

2 Complete the sentences with words from Exercise 1.

1 In many countries on April 1st people play _____ on each other.

2 The famous phone _____ last year cost a lot of people a lot of money.

3 People who obtain money through deception can be jailed for _____.

4 It is becoming increasingly common for people to make _____ claims for traffic accidents.

Listen

1 ⊙ 34.1 You are going to listen to a phone conversation. Listen and complete the information.

The phone call is from the (1) _____. It is to tell Mrs (2) _____ that she has won (3) _____ prize in the (4) _____ lottery. Her prize money is (5) _____. The accounts department needs to know her (6) _____ so that they can (7) _____ her money. Before they can release the money, they need her to send them (8) £ _____ to cover the (9) _____. If she had won first prize, she would have received (10) £ _____.

1 I am delighted to _____

2 a _____ cash sum

3 he will talk _____

4 I understand congratulations are _____

5 I'm still _____ from the shock.

6 Can I take a _____?

7 within a _____

8 the insurance _____

Talk about it

1 Work in pairs. Discuss the questions.

1 What is reassuring about the phone call?

2 What is suspicious about the phone call?

2 Imagine you receive this text on your mobile. What could the catch be? Should you phone the number?

> Mrs. Parker you have won third prize in an International Lottery. Contact this number immediately for information about the prize.

Read about it

1 Read the article about the famous Eiffel Tower Hoax of 1925.

Tower for sale

In 1925 a notorious con artist, Victor Lustig, developed a plan to sell the Eiffel Tower for scrap. At the time it was not implausible as the Tower had never been intended to be a permanent monument and it was very expensive to maintain. Lustig invited six scrap dealers to a confidential meeting at a prestigious Paris hotel. He asked for bids and when the winner became suspicious he pretended to be a corrupt official who was looking for extra money. The victim, a M. Poisson, found this story wholly believable and handed over not only the money for the Tower but also a bribe. Lustig and his accomplice left Paris with the money in a suitcase before the victim could contact the government department for further details. When M. Poisson eventually discovered he was the victim of a major hoax, he was too embarrassed to report Lustig to the police!

2 Find words in the article with these meanings.

1 completely _____

2 unbelievable _____

3 gave _____

4 famous _____

5 secret _____

3 Work in pairs. Do you know of any famous hoaxes? Tell each other about any you have heard of.

Write about it

1 Work in pairs. Plan a scam or a hoax. Write a dialogue for this like the one on the recording, or write an article about it.

2 Tell the class about your scam or hoax. Whose idea is the craziest/funniest/most plausible or most ridiculous?

Undercover

Lead in

Work in pairs. Discuss these questions.

- Write down as many professions as you can in two minutes. Are people from these professions generally admired or not? Why?

- Which professions have had a dubious reputation in the past? Why?

Word work

1 Look at the adjectives in the box. Check differences in meaning in the dictionary.

> dishonest disreputable devious
> aggressive bullying shady underhand
> corrupt ruthless pushy dodgy

2 Give an example of what a person with each of the characteristics might do.

Read about it

1 **What do you know about the work of a private investigator? Think about these things.**

- advantages and disadvantages of the job

- the type of work they do

- qualities needed to be a good private investigator (PI)

2 a **You are going to read a magazine article about the job of a PI. What questions would you like to be answered in the article?**

b **Read the article on page 73. Does it answer your questions?**

3 **Read the article again and decide if the statements are true (T) or false (F).**

1 Private Investigators live up to their image.

2 They have training.

3 They are allowed to break the law sometimes.

4 They aren't paid very well.

5 They often work for famous people.

6 They usually tell people things they already know.

4 **Choose correct meaning for these words from the article, a or b.**

		a	**b**
1	dingy	**a** dark and dirty	**b** with a bad smell
2	cluttered	**a** well organised	**b** too full and untidy
3	shabby	**a** dirty	**b** not new
4	wrinkled	**a** creased	**b** with holes in
5	shake off	**a** lose	**b** follow
6	in demand	**a** asked a lot of questions	**b** wanted
7	trustworthy	**a** can keep a secret	**b** believes what they're told
8	confidential	**a** secret	**b** organised
9	adhere to	**a** avoid	**b** stick to
10	harbour	**a** keep inside	**b** tell

My Job

A man sits in a dingy, cluttered office. His feet are on the desk, his hat pulled down over his face. His shabby suit is wrinkled and he looks as if he has been up all night. A half-smoked cigarette droops from his mouth and his hand holds an empty whisky glass. This is a scene from a dozen old private eye movies and is a seedy image that the profession is still trying to shake off. The reality couldn't be further from the truth. And I should know, I've been a PI for over ten years now. I don't smoke and only drink in moderation. I'm well-trained, well-dressed and very much in demand. I also stick to what's legal.

People often ask why I've chosen to do such a badly-paid, unskilled job. In fact, we don't come cheap! Surveillance, which takes up the main part of our job, can cost several hundred pounds an hour, so it's basically the wealthy, high-profile celebrities who employ us. Of course, another reason these people become our clients is that we are totally trustworthy and keep everything confidential. In addition to this, PIs need to have many skills. Firstly, we have to be trained in sophisticated surveillance techniques. These include following targets over fairly long periods, working in teams of at least three people and using motorbikes and/or specially adapted vehicles. And of course, we have to be trained to use the specialist electronic and photographic equipment that is part and parcel of the job. And it's not all about hidden cameras. We have to be able to follow paper trails and search records to trace missing people.

Do we ever break the law? Well, sometimes we get close. There are, however, strict legal guidelines that we have to follow if we want to keep our licenses. We adhere to these really strictly, otherwise we risk prosecution ourselves. We have to know exactly how far we can go. For example, because of data protection laws we can't find the names of people from their mobile phone numbers. And however we are portrayed on film, we can't break and enter for any reason at all. The old idea that the PI will do anything because 'the end justifies the means' just doesn't wash today!

The sort of work we do is more varied than people think, too. Most people imagine that we get hired mainly for matrimonial jobs – when someone wants to find out whether their partner is having an affair. To tell the truth, it's confirmation they really want. Most of these people are already suspicious and our job is to prove that their suspicions are right and get evidence they can use, either to win their spouse back or take them for a fortune in the divorce courts. But these cases only make up about fifty percent of a PI's caseload. We're also hired by clients who want to check out people's backgrounds – to prove they are who they say they are. And a really rewarding part of the job is tracing missing people.

In my years in the job, I've been hired by newspapers, solicitors and insurance companies as well as the odd celebrity. Even big businesses sometimes call on people like me to check out their employees – to see whether they're attending the meetings they're supposed to be attending! It seems that as long as people continue to harbour distrust, suspicion and insecurity, I'm never going to be out of a job. Unlike a lot of my clients!

5

a Match words 1–7 with words a–g to make expressions connected to a PI's work.

1	under	a	someone's background
2	put	b	surveillance
3	confirm	c	evidence
4	check out	d	a tail on
5	tracking	e	a missing person
6	trace	f	suspicions
7	collect	g	device

b Work in pairs. Study the collocations for a minute and then test each other.

Write about it

1 **Imagine you hire a PI to check on someone. Supply the PI with a list of the person's expected routine activities during the day.**

2 **Exchange the list with another student. Imagine you are the PI. You have tailed the target for a day and you write a report. You should include any departures from normal routine and any suspicious circumstances. Remember these points.**

- You will need to use narrative tenses (e.g. *Mr X left his home at …*).
- You will need to use time expressions and sequencing words (e.g. *at 2.30 precisely, five minutes later, after,* etc.).

Dangerous **fun**

Lead in

Work in pairs. Discuss these questions.

- Do you do anything you would consider to be dangerous?
- What are *health and safety regulations*? Give some examples.
- What would these regulations be for the place you are in today?
- How important is it to have regulations like these for the workplace or public places?
- In your country are there any television programmes that show dangerous stunts?

Read about it

1 Read the newspaper article and answer the questions.

Dangerous driving?

A top TV programme with over five million viewers features three presenters discussing cars. It is called *Top Gear* and is one of the most popular programmes on BBC 2. In this programme the presenters do not simply discuss the cars in front of a studio audience – they also test drive them and do outrageous stunts such as racing cars against trains, planes and speedboats. They are concerned with the fun and thrill of driving and certainly not with the environmental or safety aspects of driving, even mocking 'boring safe' drivers. The show has a huge following of fans who love speed and want to experience a vicarious thrill – given that they themselves do not have the opportunity to drive at speeds of over 70 mph in the UK. However, recently the whole future of *Top Gear* and similar programmes has been called into question after one of the presenters only just survived a crash when travelling close to 300 mph while apparently attempting to break the world land speed record. Many issues have been raised concerning health and safety regulations and whether programmes such as this should be allowed to show people taking risks in this way. If such programmes are banned or toned down, it would be a huge disappointment to the viewers and yet another example of how 'the powers that be' are becoming far too overprotective and in the process cutting out a lot of what makes life fun. As a journalist recently remarked, many people believe that personal risk should be a matter between a man and his insurance company. Otherwise, where do you draw the line?

1 What happens on the programme?

2 Why do people enjoy watching it?

3 What happened recently?

4 What effect might this have on the future of the programme and others like it? Why?

5 What is the attitude of the writer of the article?

2 Find words or phrases in the newspaper article to match the definitions.

1 people who support a person or point of view _____

2 the people in charge _____

3 no longer allowed _____

4 when the advisability of something is doubted _____

5 unbelievable and shocking _____

6 points for discussion _____

7 when you don't do something yourself but watch someone else do it _____

8 made less extreme/exciting _____

Talk about it

1 Work in pairs. Discuss and note down points to support an opposing view to the one given in the last part of the article on page 74.

2 As a class, discuss this question.

- Should programmes that feature excessively dangerous activities be shown on television?

Write about it

1 Look at the contrasting language used in these sentences to express an opposing point of view and then finish the sentences.

1 Although many people maintain that passive smoking does not necessarily lead to lung problems, many experts …

2 We like to think that we're doing as much as we can to help the environment but in reality …

3 In spite of assertions by the Government that more money will be put into public transport, it now seems …

4 Exam results in the UK indicate that standards are rising in schools. Teachers, however, insist that …

2 Choose one phrase from each group write a follow-up sentence for one of the sentences in Exercise 1.

Recent events have shown …   The last few years have seen …
There is currently an important debate in progress about …

What concerns me is …
We should not lose sight of …

I would like to address some of the issues …   I intend to look at points in favour and against …

The vast majority of people …
A tiny minority …   The silent majority …

It is a well/little known fact that …
Most people are aware of the fact that …

3 Write a discursive essay with the title 'Should programmes that feature excessively dangerous activities be shown on television?' Use the guide to help you structure your essay.

- Introduction: outline the controversy
- Present reasons for
- Present reasons against
- Draw a conclusion

Leave those
kids alone

Lead in

Work in pairs. Discuss these questions.

- Did you enjoy your first school? Why/Why not?
- Can children today do the same things as you did at school? Think about these things

  playground games   lessons
  sports   food   discipline
  drama   getting to school
  clothes   jewellery

Read about it

Read the article and match the comments 1–7 with the two points of view, A and B.

In recent years life for children at primary school in the UK has changed a great deal. The concern of the Government for the welfare of our children has meant the implementation of various rules and guidelines that have made the headlines. Some of these have been instigated by local councils and individual boards of governors as opposed to the Government but all have contributed to the overall consensus of opinion that our schools are becoming very different places from those the previous generation attended. (A) Many applaud this concern and welcome any measures that can afford our children additional protection. However, (B) many ridicule the rules as being excessively protective and an interference by the 'Nanny State'.

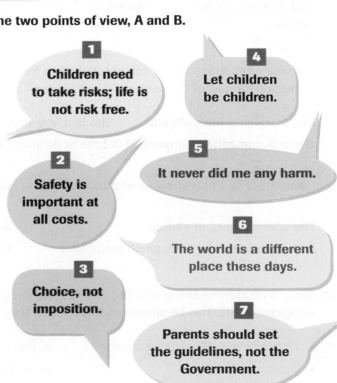

1 Children need to take risks; life is not risk free.

2 Safety is important at all costs.

3 Choice, not imposition.

4 Let children be children.

5 It never did me any harm.

6 The world is a different place these days.

7 Parents should set the guidelines, not the Government.

Word work

1 **Make nouns from the verbs in the box. Which words keep the same form?**

> applaud   implement   impose   instigate   interfere   ridicule   concern
> contribute   protect   welcome

2 **Complete the sentences with words from Exercise 1.**

1 His failure was held up to _____.

2 He made a fine _____ to the debate.

3 The government _____ a large fine on those councils that refused to _____ the new regulations.

4 At the award ceremony she was _____ for her continued success.

5 He stole the money but it was his brother who _____ the crime.

Talk about it

1 **Read the rules. Which ones were applied in your primary school?**

School Rules

1 No junk food allowed at school.

2 No photos to be taken of school plays or sports days.

3 No running games allowed in the playground.

4 No games of 'conkers' permitted on school premises.

5 No smacking allowed.

6 No toy guns allowed in school.

7 Teachers are not permitted to put sun cream on children.

8 Children are not allowed to wear any make up or jewellery to school.

9 The word 'failure' is not to be used in school.

10 Children are not allowed to use any playground climbing equipment unsupervised.

11 Children are not allowed outside in wet or very hot weather.

2 **Work in pairs. Look at the rules in Exercise 1 and discuss the questions.**

1 Why do you think these rules were brought in?

2 Do you think these are good rules? Why/Why not?

3 Which rules do you think should be changed?

4 Are there any rules you would like to introduce? Why?

3 **Work in pairs. Discuss the questions.**

1 In what other ways are we more 'protected' in society than we used to be?

2 Do you think we will experience more or less freedom in the future?

3 Do you think we live in a safer society than we used to? Why/Why not?

> **Useful language**
> In all probablitity …   This is ridiculous!
> I think it's fair enough to say …
> This is going too far.   OK, I accept that … but …

Write about it

Write a description of how school life has changed in your country in the last ten years. Refer to your discussion at the beginning of this unit. Think about these things.

- what life was like then
- what life is like now
- which changes you think are for the better/worse
- how you think it may change in the future

What's the score?

Lead in

1 Work in pairs. Discuss these questions.

- When you see a film do you usually notice or remember the score?
- What's your favourite film score or soundtrack?
- What can music add to a film?
- Can you name any TV theme tunes that you would immediately recognise?
- Can you hum one to your partner?

2 Try to name a film or TV programme for each category in the box. Do they have a memorable score or soundtrack?

1 horror	**6** animation
2 action	**7** superhero
3 romantic	**8** war
4 chick flick	**9** comedy
5 sci-fi	

Word work

Complete the sentences with the best word, a, b, c or d.

1 I'm a terrible singer. I'm always out of _____.
   a notes   **b** tune   **c** melody   **d** song

2 My granddad can't _____ very well because of his false teeth.
   a whistle   **b** hum   **c** sing   **d** belt out

3 It's beautiful, _____ music.
   a discordant   **b** catchy   **c** singalong   **d** haunting

4 My favourite _____ is Mozart.
   a musician   **b** composer   **c** singer   **d** artist

5 The film is an absolute _____.
   a attraction   **b** perfection   **c** masterpiece   **d** hit

6 He wrote the _____ of my favourite song. I listen to it every day.
   a script   **b** score   **c** lyrics   **d** poem

Listen

1 One of the most famous film scores is for the film *Psycho*. Work in small groups and answer the questions.

   1 What does *Psycho* mean?

   2 Have you seen the original 1960 film *Psycho*?

   3 Who directed it?

   4 Do you know anything about the story?

2 🔊 **38.1** Listen to the synopsis of *Psycho* and match the names 1–6 with the people a–f.

1 Sam Loomis	**a** the woman who dies
2 Bates	**b** the woman's sister
3 Marion Crane	**c** the woman's boyfriend
4 Lila	**d** the person who runs the motel
5 Milton	**e** the name of the motel
6 Norman	**f** the private investigator

3 🔊 **38.1** Complete the text with words from the box. Listen again to check.

> mummified   rage   adjacent
> embezzles   bedridden   horrified
> distract   identity   traps   isolated
> shadowy   suspicious   basement

4 Which tenses are used to tell the story?

Films

The film tells the story of Marion Crane, a young woman who is in love with a guy called Sam Loomis. She (1) _____ money from her boss so that she and Sam can be together. Marion runs away and ends up at an (2) _____ motel called the Bates Motel which is run by a young man called Norman. Norman lives in an old mansion (3) _____ to the hotel with his (4) _____ mother. Marion takes a room at the motel and over dinner she and Norman discuss life and its (5) _____. Marion decides to go back and return the money but she doesn't have the chance. That night she is stabbed to death while in the shower by a (6) _____ figure that looks like an old lady. Norman discovers the body and is (7) _____. He hides the body and cleans up after the murder to protect his mother. Other people arrive at the Bates Motel looking for Marion. A private investigator comes first and is stabbed on the stairs in the mansion. Then Marion's boyfriend, Sam, arrives with her sister, Lila, and they discover that in fact Norman's mother died several years ago. While Sam tries to (8) _____ Norman, Lila goes to search the mansion. She goes down to the (9) _____ where she finds the (10) _____ corpse of an old lady. Meanwhile, Norman becomes (11) _____ and knocks Sam out. He goes up to the mansion. Suddenly 'Mother' comes up behind Lila. Sam arrives on the scene just in time to save Lila and they find that 'Mother' is in fact Norman, dressed in his mother's clothes. Later at the police station we learn that Norman killed his mother in a jealous (12) _____ and since then he has kept his mother 'alive' by taking on her (13) _____. He has shut out any memory of what really happened. The film finishes with Norman alone in his cell.

Write about it

The soundtrack or score for *Psycho* is very famous. Soundtracks are an important part of what makes a movie memorable.

1 🔊 **38.2** Listen to two short pieces of soundtracks for silent movies from the early 1900s. Match the music and functions.

1 'hurry' music   **2** 'death' music

2 Work in pairs. Write a short synopsis of the action that the music describes. Remember to use present tenses.

Let it all **out**

Lead in

Work in pairs. When did you last do these things? Answer the questions.

> split your sides really let rip
> have a good blub
> shoot your mouth off

- When did it happen?
- Where did it happen?
- Why did it happen?
- How did you feel afterwards?

Word work

1 **Look at the phrases in the box. Are they related to laughter (L), anger (A), embarrassment (E) or showing your feelings (S)?**

> creased up lose it to be in fits
> blow your top get it off your chest
> I could've died freak out get the giggles
> show your true colours burst a blood vessel
> wear your heart on your sleeve have a good rant

2 **Work in pairs. Take it in turns to choose a phrase from Exercise 1 and get your partner to describe a situation to illustrate it.**

Talk about it

Work in pairs. Discuss these questions.

- Do you cry very often?
- What makes you cry?
- Does crying make you feel better or worse?
- 'Big boys don't cry!' Would you ever say this to a child? Why/Why not?
- Do you think it is acceptable for men to cry these days? In what circumstances?

1 Read the article and answer the questions.

Big boys do cry

How do you feel if you see a guy well up at the end of a sad movie? Or if there's a man in obvious distress trying heroically to keep a lid on his emotions? Do you think 'Go on. Have a good cry, you'll feel better,' and offer a tissue or do you think, 'That's not right. Men don't cry.' According to recent research, it is now quite acceptable for guys to cry. Whereas in the past moist-eyed males were considered weak and over sensitive, now it seems that the occasional solitary tear only adds to a man's masculinity. It must be said, however, that full on blubbing is still a definite turn off.

Apparently this change of image is down to a certain number of men in the public eye who have recently shed a tear or two. These are men who would normally be classed as 'the strong, silent type', very much a man's man. Remember David Beckham's tears after the 2006 world cup? And going back a while, Paul Gascoigne, another footballer, cried openly in a well-televised match. In fact footballers can be seen weeping quite regularly after losing an important match. The more cynical among us might well put this down to a potential loss of earnings but, generally speaking, they are showing true emotion.

Politicians, another group of strong, self-disciplined men, do not actually turn on the waterworks but sometimes allow a restrained tear to roll down a cheek when facing tragic circumstances. We, the watching public, think 'Yes, that's OK. It shows he cares.'

So have attitudes to men's tears really changed? Psychologists say that they have. It can be manly to cry depending on two things: the situation must warrant it and the crying should be restrained. It is apparently also even a fact that in the right circumstances a man's tears can receive more sympathy than a woman's. Is this all about image? Or is this a sign of the more general tendency today of not bottling up our emotions? We'd like to know your opinions. Log on to our website and let us know what you think.

1 How many words connected with crying can you find in the article?

2 How many words connected with 'man' are there in the article?

2 Read the article again and decide if the statements are true (T) or false (F).

1 Uncontrolled crying gains a lot of sympathy.

2 Paul Gasgoigne cried recently at a football match.

3 Footballers who cry might be worrying about their money.

4 The public reaction to politicians' tears is positive.

5 Women who cry can receive less sympathy than men.

6 Nowadays it is common to let our emotions show.

Write a comment (50–100 words) expressing your opinion to post on the magazine's website.

Shopped **out**

Lead in

1 Work in pairs. Discuss these questions.

- When did you last go shopping?
- Where did you go?
- What did you buy?

2 Complete the questionnaire opposite and compare your answers with another student.

3 Work in pairs. What do you think are the most important things for the people in the pictures when they shop? Discuss your ideas.

Spending habits

1 Where do you prefer to shop and why?

2 Do you prefer to go shopping alone? Why/Why not?

3 Do you ever buy or sell items over the Internet?

4 Do you ever buy second-hand items?

5 Have you ever been to a car boot sale or a jumble sale?

6 What, if anything, do you buy from street vendors?

7 What are the most important things for you when you are shopping (quality, cost, convenience, etc.)?

Word work

Look at the list of places in the box. What sort of things can you buy in these places and which of them do you have near where you live?

> mall   car boot sale   street market
> discount store   charity shop   covered markets
> shopping arcade   kiosk   department store
> pound store   jumble sale   garage sale
> second hand shop   catalogue shop   stall
> fete   mobile stall

Read about it

1 Read a report on a new shopping mall and answer the questions.

1 What positive points came out of the survey?

2 What were the negative points?

3 Which concerns are not addressed in the writer's recommendations?

2 Find these verbs in the report. How are they used? Why are some in the passive form?

> ask   question   find   mention   praise   express
> make a request   note   consider   display

Report on the Tyndell Shopping Mall

The aim of this report is to improve the shopping experience for visitors to the new Tyndell Shopping Mall and is based on a survey carried out over a week-long period by a team of three at the main entrance to the Mall. Questions were asked concerning visitors' reactions to the design and layout of the Mall, the range of shops and services and the means of transport used to get to and from the Mall.

Design and layout

Most of those questioned were impressed by the modern design and generally found the layout simple and easy to negotiate. Many mentioned the overall impression of space given by the high roof and wide walkways for shoppers. The cleanliness and freshness of the atmosphere, helped by the use of plants and trees, was also praised. A number of people expressed a desire for more Mall maps to be displayed by the escalators and a request was also made for Mall staff to be available for enquiries. A few older members of the public would like to have more lifts to facilitate movement between levels.

Range of shops and services

The vast majority of those surveyed thought the range of shops and services was excellent. They were particularly happy with the number and variety of restaurants on the second floor. However, a significant number mentioned the lack of a coffee shop on the ground floor. It was also noted by a large number of people that the toilet facilities are minimal.

Transport

It appears that most visitors come to the Mall by car and are happy with the amount of parking provided in the underground car park, although most considered the parking fees excessive. Those who travelled to the Mall by bus were happy with the service and the closeness of the stops to the Mall's main entrance.

Conclusion and Recommendations

The results of the survey show quite clearly that in general visitors to the Mall are impressed by the design and range of shops and services. The provision of a coffee shop or refreshment area needs to be addressed quickly as does the extension of toilet facilities. Additionally, more Mall maps should be displayed throughout the Mall and the presence of Mall staff at key points on all floors for at least the first few months would be very helpful to visitors. It would also be advisable to hold off any increases in parking fees for the foreseeable future. These recommendations are all feasible and would contribute to a better shopping experience for visitors to the Mall.

3 Find formal equivalents for the <u>underlined</u> words in in the report.

1 We must <u>deal with</u> these points.

2 It would be <u>a good idea</u>.

3 It's a <u>realistic</u> solution.

4 Nothing is going to happen in the <u>months ahead</u>.

5 It will <u>make</u> parking <u>easier</u>.

4 Find and <u>underline</u> the phrases in the report that contain the words in the box.

aim	based	questions	most
number of	vast majority		significant
	noted		

Write about it

1 Work in pairs. Think of an imaginary new shopping mall or shopping website. Note down positive and negative comments from an imaginary survey.

2 Write a report based on your comments from Exercise 1. Remember these points about reports.

- they use formal language
- they usually focus on facts
- they are usually impersonal and use passive forms

Recording scripts

UNIT 1

 1.1

1 What d'you think about working from home?

2 How d'you feel about working abroad?

3 I think that would be really difficult. How about you?

4 Don't you think it would be better to go to university?

UNIT 2

 2.1

I really enjoyed our conversation.

 2.2

1 Nothing on tonight? Treat yourself to pieces of heaven in a box. Moonlight Magic. Chocolates to die for.

2 Final countdown! Last day to grab those bargains! Get along to Carpet Stores for fantastic savings on all leading makes! Don't miss out. You'll be amazed by our prices. Hurry to Carpet Stores Winter Sale – NOW!

3 Your hair spoiling your social life? Fed up with tangles and split ends? Spending a fortune at the hairdresser's? Well, stop right there! Our new formula, Revelle 5, will save you time **and** money. Say goodbye to dry hair with Revelle 5 shampoo and conditioner. Let **us** help **you**.

4 **A:** He's done it again! Mud from the football pitch, tomato sauce from dinner, grass from fighting with his sister! Just how am I expected to get these things clean?

B: You obviously haven't heard about our new, improved Whitestar washing powder. Guaranteed to remove any stain your young hooligan can come up with! Try it and see. Perfect results or your money back. Whitestar washing powder, light years ahead of its time.

5 Sleek, sexy, with all the curves in the right places and a purring performance to outdistance all the competition. The new Panther saloon. Stay in front.

6 That time of year again? Insurance renewal. Scratching your head over the maze of offers out there? Insurance Direct offers you easy, fast, no fuss quotations over the phone. We are the best – contact us now! For all your insurance needs from health to holidays, pets to property, call us on 0800 77 66 2381. That's 0800 77 66 2381.

UNIT 6

 6.1

1 I'll do **all** your laundry for a **month** if you say yes!

2 The film was **rubbish**, the coffee was **cold** and it was **freezing** in the cinema.

3 He has **no tact** at all when he's talking to people.

4 I cannot **believe** he did that to you. Wait till I see him! My brother is the **biggest cheater** on this planet and I'm sick of him thinking he can just treat every girl he goes out with so badly. You wait till I tell **Mum** about this latest incident.

5 Weather's **brilliant** again, isn't it? What did you get up to **yesterday** then?

6 You're about the most **intelligent** guy I've met in **years**. A **first** from Cambridge – that's **amazing**. Tell me about your **research** in that lovely **Ferrari** of yours.

6.2

I = Interviewer, **S** = Suzie Rogers

I: On today's programme our guest is psychologist Susie Rogers and we're discussing Helen Haynes's new book with the interesting title *Gossip is Good for You*. Hello Susie.

S: Hello.

I: So, this title *Gossip is Good for You* … I think most people will be behind me when I say that surely 'gossip' by its very nature implies that people are saying bad things about other people when they're not there to defend themselves. What 'good' can there be in that?

S: You see – you're falling into the trap of thinking that all gossip is negative. It's not! Only about five percent of gossip is dissing other people.

I: You obviously haven't been in our canteen when the boss is away!

S: But that's healthy, you see. You're getting rid of your frustrations and at the same time you're bonding with your colleagues – and that's good.

I: So it's all about bonding?

S: Yes, they say that since we've had language the human race has always had a form of gossip. It's connected with building relationships, making social rules, establishing status, sharing opinions and making us feel accepted and part of society.

I: So, me saying that my boss is a creepy, arrogant old … (only an example Robert – you're a sweetie really) is going to help me feel part of the group.

S: If the others share your opinion, yes. But remember, gossip is not always bad. We gossip about ourselves, our experiences and family. We use gossip to get and give advice. We exchange social information.

I: Right. So when I say, 'Hey Fran, who was that gorgeous guy I saw you with outside your house yesterday?' And she says, 'That's my new plumber.' We're exchanging social information.

S: Exactly. And an important feel-good factor about gossiping is that it releases endorphins.

I: Endorphins?

S: You know – natural painkillers. It makes you more relaxed, reduces the heart rate and gets rid of stress. You really do feel better after a good goss!

I: And the big question – do women really gossip more than men?

S: Well the statistics show – no, not really. There's very little difference. The main difference is that men gossip more about their **own** relationships and women are more keen to admit that they gossip whereas men usually deny it completely.

I: Well thanks Susie. A revelation. Our time is up, we have to finish but just before you go – who **was** that gorgeous woman you were talking to just before we came on air …

 6.3

A: You'll never guess what I heard on the train this morning.

B: Go on!

A: Apparently, they're going to treble the prices on some routes!

B: You're joking!

A: And they're going to charge extra if you're over a certain weight!

B: Now, come on – that's got to be a wind up!

A: No way – the woman that's married to the tall ticket inspector told the guy who runs the café. And he told my friend Bill.

UNIT 8

 8.1

1 One person can't make a difference.

2 What's the point?

3 It's time the silent majority spoke up.

4 Leave it to the politicians. They know what they're doing.

5 I'll go along with whatever you decide.

6 Why bother. It's pointless.

7 If everyone thought like you, nothing would ever get done.

8 I couldn't care less.

9 People are so apathetic these days.

10 No one else cares. Why should I?

11 If everyone did their bit, we could really change things.

12 We need to make our feelings known, if just for our own conscience.

UNIT 10

 10.1

A: Cheer up!

B: Why should I?

A: Look on the bright side!

B: There isn't one.

A: It can't be that bad!

B: On no?

A: It's not the end of the world!

B: What do you know about it?

A: I know how to put a smile on your face!

 10.2

K = Kelly, **B** = Bev

B: Hello?

K: Hi Bev.

B: Hi Kelly. You sound a bit low.

K: At least I can be myself when I'm talking to you.

B: What are you talking about?

K: I think the technical term is 'emotional labour'. I've been emotionally labouring all day.

B: Now you really have lost me.

K: According to this programme I heard the other day, it's 'faking it' – showing emotions you don't feel or hiding ones that you do. I've been smiling all day long – with this cheesy grin fixed on my face – when in reality I feel awful.

B: OK. I know what you're talking about. I've heard about it, too. It's called 'have a nice day syndrome' where everyone at work is expected to be relentlessly cheerful or …

K: … they get ticked off by the boss like I was today.

B: You weren't!

K: Apparently, I wasn't smiling in the right way! We've had e-mails and leaflets – even a seminar – about using the right body language and tone of voice. We're supposed to be perky, pleasant and relaxed 100% of the time!

B: It's crazy. I can understand them not wanting us to be walking round looking like we've got the weight of the world on our shoulders all the time. But sticking on a fake smile when you're feeling like death warmed up is not the answer.

K: Tell me about it! Then, of course, when I get home I take it out on poor Tom. Perhaps I ought to change jobs.

B: To be what? An undertaker?!

10.3

1   Now you really have lost me!

2   OK.

3   You weren't!

4   It's crazy!

5   Tell me about it!

 10.4

A: A lot of people think that the term 'emotional labour' is just an empty piece of jargon but it really does exist. It's a modern condition and it describes what happens when people fake or hide emotions in order to appear pleasant and relaxed to those around them. It was first recognised when studies were made of flight attendants in the 1970s and it was found that the most important part of their job was being able to hide their irritation. Now every workplace requires its workers to be constantly happy.

B: But this is nothing new, surely? And isn't it just common sense? No customer is going to want to deal with staff who are gloomy and have long faces all the time.

A: To an extent you're right. We all 'fake it' a lot of the time. It's how we get on with other people. But constantly faking emotions can take its toll. You need a lot of energy to control emotion. People who are doing this all day long can get exhausted.

B: Yes – smiling must be very tiring – all those muscles you're using!

A: It's not just that. We all need the chance to be ourselves – say what we feel, vent our emotions. Otherwise we end up completely numb – unable to feel anything at all. This obviously has a knock-on effect on the family. Going from happy employee to happy wife and happy mum can literally make you ill!

B: Isn't this all just psycho babble?

A: I don't think it is. We're under so much pressure these days to be the perfect employee, the perfect spouse, the perfect parent that people are just feeling guilty all the time that they can't live up to what's expected of them. So we lie. And one way we lie is by faking our emotions.

B: I still think this is pretty normal stuff. Look at shop assistants. The ones I see are usually lazy, bored and more concerned about discussing their nails or their partners with their colleagues than dealing with the needs of the customers. They're certainly not faking anything!

A: Maybe they're not paid enough to care!

UNIT 13

 13.1

A: I can't believe the way they report the news in this country!

B: What are you moaning about now?

A: Did you realise that David Beckam got top slot on the News at Seven today. His story had priority over two soldiers who were killed in the Middle East.

B: Well, Beckham's very popular here.

A: That's not the point. He's a footballer for goodness sake. He shouldn't get priority over military action.

B: Yeah, I know what you're saying but surely the news guys have to go with what's going to interest most people?

A: No. They've got a duty to keep us informed of the most important things. And another thing – why don't you see much international news on your TV? People here can't have any idea of what's happening in the rest of the world. You are so insular! You really need to get your priorities right!

UNIT 14

 **14.1**

A It's just so reassuring to know that I can find out where she is at any time. We can track her movements through this new system. It's amazing – as long as she has it switched on! These days it's so important to know where they are and that they're safe – you worry so much if they're late. Life is so dangerous these days – this just takes such a load off your mind!

B I can't stand it. I think it's simply appalling. You can't go anywhere in this town without being caught on film. Whatever happened to privacy? George Orwell got it just right. Big Brother is watching us. Soon it'll be in our homes as well and then there'll be no escape at all.

C No way. These checks have gone too far. I mean, photos fine but eye prints? Thumb prints? And as for having all this information in one place – that's just asking for trouble. Identity theft is such a problem today – more sophisticated ways of recording the information isn't going to stop the thieves. They'll simply up their game. And with these new cards we're handing them everything on a plate! They're going to be compulsory, too! Crazy.

D Yeah. I totally agree. Test everyone and have it on record. Finger prints, too. Help beat crime. No problem. Safety first, that's what I say.

E No. I think the laws controlling this are nowhere near tight enough. I mean, it's the ultimate invasion of privacy, isn't it. I think the police or secret service or whatever need really strong grounds to do it.

 **14.2**

A It's just so reassuring to know that I can find out where she is at any time.
It's amazing.
These days it's so important to know where they are and that they're safe.
Life is so dangerous these days.

B I can't stand it.
I think it's simply appalling.
You can't go anywhere in this town without being caught on film.
Big Brother is watching us.

C These checks have gone too far.
I mean, photos fine but eye prints? Thumb prints? And as for having all this information in one place – that's just asking for trouble.

D I totally agree.

E No. I think the laws controlling this are nowhere near tight enough.

UNIT 17

 17.1

J = James, **R** = Ruth

R: Hi James.

J: Ruth, my favourite niece! You said you had an idea you wanted to talk over.

R: Well, I need some advice and I'd like to borrow some money! So, who better to come to than the businessman in the family!

J: If I can help, I will. Tell me about it.

R: I've decided to take a bit of a risk and start my own business. I'm looking for a backer.

J: That's good news. I've always thought you'd have a good head for business. So run this idea past me. If it's any good, I'll see if I can help with the finance.

R: I've decided to open a beauty salon in the town centre.

J: Have you done your research?

R: Oh yes. It's an ideal business project. There's very little competition in the area. I've done a lot of surveys and it seems that there's a great demand for the type of salon that I have in mind. I reckon I could get a good return on my initial outlay within eighteen months.

J: It sounds like you've really thought this through.

R: I have. It would be an excellent investment for you. I can practically guarantee …

J: OK. Let's not get carried away. Tell me a bit more about the project. Why do you think it would be so popular, what would be your running costs, etcetera, then we'll talk money.

UNIT 18

 **18.1**

S = Simon, **L** = Lizzie

S: I was in the supermarket earlier today and they were playing this awful, syrupy music. It nearly put me off my shopping! I mean, who wants to listen to stuff like that while you're trying to choose your baked beans!

L: Oh come on, Simon! Most people like background music …

S: Well I think all background music – canned, piped, musak, whatever you want to call it – should be banned. It's really bad.

L: So, you don't like it then.

S: No, Lizzie, I don't. You know me, I love music. It's just it has to be in its place and when I've got control of the on/off switch. What I don't like is listening to loud raucous music while I'm choosing clothes or irritating soft syrupy tunes when I'm in the chemist waiting for a prescription.

L: You're going a bit over the top there. And by the way, it's called easy listening music.

S: Whatever it's called, I prefer silence, thank you very much.

L: Well, you're in a minority. Most people love to have music around them. And don't you think in some places it can really add to the atmosphere? I mean, when I'm clothes shopping, if there's good music playing, it puts me in a good mood.

S: Yeah – it puts you in the mood for spending money.

L: So? Advertisers target us all the time – at least with music it's making the experience more enjoyable.

S: That's a matter of opinion.

L: Seriously, aren't there some places you don't mind it?

S: I suppose it's OK in some restaurants – as long as it's not completely in your face.

L: See.

S: And there must be some places you don't like it?

L: Well, to be honest, I can't stand the music they play when you're holding on the phone. Nothing worse than having Abba singing *Waterloo* again and again – and again!

S: Hey, don't knock Abba! At least they're better than some of the music you can get stuck with for half an hour. And you can't agree with this idea to put televisions and piped music on long distance trains.

L: Yeah, I'd heard about that. That would be terrible. On trains you're completely trapped.

S: Yeah. At least with shops and phones you can hang up or leave. Why on earth they want to make us watch TVs on trains – well, that's completely beyond me.

L: Apparently it's something to do with breaking the monotony, letting people catch up with the news or something.

S: But most guys I know just want to read their books or papers or doze off for a while. **And** they're talking about having background music in hospitals.

L: That's OK. They can be pretty gloomy places anyway and it might take people's minds off their problems. It might actually be good for people, make them less anxious.

S: See – that's where we differ. I think everyone has the right to silence. If you want music, bring your own.

L: Oh you are such a killjoy! Music pleases so many people. Think how awful a completely silent world would be.

S: You're twisting my words. That's **not** what I said. Music has its place. But that is not in shops, tube stations or in hospitals.

L: OK – I think you've made your point!

18.2

1   What I don't like is travelling on a crowded train.

2   There's nothing worse than when the phone rings in the middle of the night.

3   Don't knock The Rolling Stones.

4   Don't you think that the rich should pay higher taxes?

5   Apparently, it's illegal in France.

6   They're talking about raising the age for buying cigarettes.

 18.3

T = Tony, **D** = Denise

T: In my opinion all mobile phones on trains should be banned!

D: Well, I think you're in a minority.

T: Come on. Some people spend the whole journey with a phone glued to their ear.

D: Now you're exaggerating.

T: How they can have intimate conversations in front of a carriage full of people is beyond me!

D: And I suppose you've never used a mobile on a train?

T: Well, emergencies are a different matter.

D: Yeah. Like when you called me yesterday to let me know when to start cooking dinner.

UNIT 21

 21.1

B = Beth, **G** = Gemma

B: Gemma. Hi!

G: Sorry?

B: You haven't got the faintest idea, have you? Beth. Bethany Wheeler. We were at school together.

G: I don't believe it. Beth! I'd never have recognised you. Not in a million years!

B: Yeah. I know. Hair's dyed. Lost two stone. Had a nose job! It's not surprising. Whereas you – you've hardly changed at all!

G: I suppose I look pretty much the same.

B: Still with Mark Townsend?

G: No way! We split four years back. I was devastated at first but you've got to move on. I work for a bank now and I married the bank manager!

B: Wow!

G: And you?

B: No. No ties. No other half. No kids. No house. No pets. Just a motorbike!

G: You really have changed. You're nowhere near as quiet as you used to be. Swotting all the time for exams. You never had any time to come out.

B: Yeah. I really changed when I went to uni. The life and the people were so different. It was a real shock to the system. I dropped out after two terms and I haven't looked back since.

G: Good for you. You look so happy!

B: Thanks. I feel really happy. And you – have things turned out the way you expected?

G: God no! I thought I'd go to drama school, get into films and lead a wild life. And look at me – happy and contented with my bank manager! Love's a strange thing!

UNIT 22

 22.1

It was one of those days, you know, when everything just falls into place! I don't know what I'd done to deserve it and **by rights** the day should've been a disaster – but for some reason that day whoever is in control of time was on my side. I was on a two-day management training course up in Bolton for my company and I knew getting back to Southampton on the train that evening was going to be **pretty tight** – five hours at least, and with connections? I didn't even want to think about it – so I didn't and enjoyed the day as best as I could. Well, ours was the last presentation of the day and that's when my luck started. We had a strict time limit of fifteen minutes for the presentation and a buzzer sounded after exactly fifteen minutes. There were three of us and I was speaking last. The other guys were overrunning and I thought, 'There's no way we're going to beat the buzzer.' Anyway, **I did my bit** and, **no kidding**, as soon as I finished my last word, the buzzer sounded! Everyone cheered! So Pete, my colleague, and I **hot footed it** to the station with no idea of train times and there, standing at the platform, was the train we needed. We **hopped on** and ten seconds later it left. **How jammy was that?** I had to change at Manchester and Pete was staying there and by then we were **starving** so we thought we'd have a quick meal at a restaurant near the station and spend our expenses. A quick meal turned into something rather bigger and longer and by now I'd more or less given up hope of getting home that night. I **figured** I'd probably have to wake up some friend in London and **kip** on their floor. Back to the station to catch the London train. Trains went at a quarter to the hour and a quarter past. I was **bang** in between. But there was a London train – the quarter to, fifteen minutes late. My luck was holding! I got on, the train left immediately and I was off to Euston and going through a list of friends who would still be up after midnight, but at Euston the ticket guy said that if I could **make it** across London in twenty-five minutes **I stood an outside chance of** catching the last train from Waterloo. Well, I **legged it** to the tube station and incredibly a tube pulled in the moment I got to the platform – and you know how long you can wait sometimes! The same thing happened when I changed lines. Tube waiting at the platform. And finally, at Waterloo, there it was, my train, waiting just for me! What it is to have time on your side for once.

Oh yeah, and just **to round things off nicely** – when I got to Southampton I didn't have any money for a taxi to work, where I'd left my car, and just as I was about to start walking there was this friend of mine, outside the station, going in the same direction and I got a lift! **Thinking back**, if I'd been a couple of seconds later at any point in the day it wouldn't have worked. Days like that don't happen too often!

UNIT 25

 25.1

1   **A:** Single women are going to be given treatment on the NHS. How good is that?
    B: I'm not so sure. Couples should get priority, surely?

2   **A:** Apparently you get pushed right down the transplant lists for hearts and livers. That's so unfair.
    B: Is it? You can understand it, though. I mean, if you don't take care of yourself.

3   **A:** I think it's appalling! It's a miracle cure and they say it's too pricy to give people. I mean, what is research all about?
    B: But it only gives an extra six months of life.

4   **A:** Did you know that you can get a nose job on the NHS now?
    B: That's only if the size is damaging you psychologically!

5   **A:** The cutbacks are really affecting my gran. All sorts of care services are being stopped.
    B: Yes. But surely it's up to the family to help out.

 25.2

1   It's <u>scan</u>dalous that people should have to …

2   It's comp<u>lete</u>ly un<u>eth</u>ical to …

3   We <u>have</u> to be realistic.

4   You <u>can't</u> ex<u>pect</u> to …

5   Can you <u>hon</u>estly <u>say</u> that …

6   Are you <u>say</u>ing that …?

7   I'm <u>sorry</u>, I don't under<u>stand</u> what you're trying to <u>say</u>.

8   This is something I feel par<u>tic</u>ularly <u>strong</u>ly about.

UNIT 26

 **26.1**

1 Mother

I was brought up very much in a Catholic background and from a very young age was taught to consider other people. Religion doesn't really have a great influence on me now but there are by-products of it when it comes to respect. Maybe some sort of education with a discussion group would help create more respect. A lot of people just never sit down and think about it. If they had a forum where they could talk about what respect is all about, it might improve their behaviour.

2 Father

Respect to me in a family context means maintaining a balance and treating your children as adults and respecting their personalities and views. I was brought up with a pretty strict approach to social behaviour and the idea that 'manners maketh man'. I think there was an assumption in previous generations that certain people commanded respect and they didn't have to earn it: people in authority, people who wore suits and had proper jobs, and so on. That has changed and there's more of a meritocracy now and people feel you need to earn respect. But I think it might now have gone too far the other way.

3 Daughter

There are different types of younger people, there are some who are just rude and don't care what other people think or what they do and there's people who do give respect and would stand up on a bus and let older people sit down. Obviously, people of a different status get respected differently – so a police officer gets more respect than a child, people who hold important jobs or who are older get more respect than younger people. But everyone should be respected and it doesn't really matter how old you are.

4 Son

You shouldn't expect people to treat you well if you don't treat them properly. People should be polite to each other. Some people don't give as much respect as they should to their elders but some older people don't notice the world is changing and people have got a different attitude towards things.

 26.2

1 There are by-products of religion when it comes to respect.

2 If they had a forum where they could talk about what respect is all about, it might improve their behaviour.

3 There was an assumption in previous generations that certain people commanded respect and they didn't have to earn it.

4 There's more of a meritocracy now and people feel you need to earn respect.

5 People of different status get respected differently.

6 Some people don't give as much respect as they should to their elders.

UNIT 28

 **28.1**

I'm going to have a good rant here. I cannot understand why they don't put extra trains on at the height of the rush hour. It's appalling. We pay sky high prices to travel by train every day and then we're forced to stand for the whole journey, elbow to elbow with other poor commuters. The carriages are so packed they get really smelly and there's no way you can get to the buffet for a coffee – mind you, there'd be no way you could drink the coffee standing up without spilling it all over yourself and other passengers! Not the safest way to travel! By the time I get to work in the mornings, my back aches, my feet hurt, my clothes are creased and smelly and I'm so frazzled it takes ages to unwind.

 28.2

Will someone please tell me how travel agents get away with advertising holidays that are nothing like their descriptions? I've just got back from a week booked in 'a luxury hotel with sea views' and half the hotel hadn't even been built yet! It was just a shell. Our room was at the back – with a disgusting view of the building site and rubbish tip. The noise was just atrocious. There was no way we could relax in our rooms in the daytime. We had to go out from 8 a.m. to 8 p.m. And the beach was filthy and covered in litter.

Oh yes, the food at the hotel was revolting – all burgers and chips and nothing like the beautiful pictures of local food in the brochure. I'm definitely going to ask for my money back. I don't usually like to make a fuss but I'm certainly up for a fight on this one.

UNIT 29

 29.1

Good morning everyone. It's good to see you all here and I'd like to start by welcoming you to this day of seminars about ways of approaching different environmental problems. I'm not going to be talking for very long, just long enough to give you a brief introduction to the topics covered in our seminars today.

I must start by stating the obvious. We all know that what we do with our waste is a huge environmental concern, but today we're going to be focusing on a source of waste that is rapidly increasing – that of E waste. Because of the speed at which technological advances are happening, all types of electronic equipment and devices are continually updated; smaller, faster, cleverer mobile phones are constantly replacing their predecessors, as are PCs, TVs, DVDs, etcetera, etcetera. And what happens to those that are no longer needed or wanted? They are either thrown away and buried in landfill sites, poisoning the environment, or stored for future disposal. Figures show that last year over 31 million old PCs were buried and 152 million stored. That is a lot of old PCs! It's clear that this cannot continue indefinitely and a lot of research is being done into how the problem can be dealt with.

Our seminars today look at ways of approaching this problem. One answer is to recycle a percentage of these old PCs and mobile phones and later on this morning you will hear from a company that does just that. In fact since it started this company has reprocessed over two million PCs both for reuse and recycling.

Other possible solutions are more – how shall we say – creative? There are a lot of innovators out there in the world of technology and these people are coming up with interesting ways around the problem of disposal of E waste all the time. You'll be amazed at some of their suggestions. I hope I'm not pre-empting the content of the seminar but I have to mention this. Apparently, one of the more creative ideas is a circuit board made out of pasta with electronic components on it – when you're

finished with it you boil it up and the bits fall off to make disposal easier. Or there's the mobile phone case with a sunflower seed embedded in it – when you plant it, a flower grows! And let's not forget the phones made from a certain plant that decomposes when you bury it. OK, I won't give away any more surprises! You'll find out all about them later on.

I hope this has given you a taste of the range of topics that you'll be hearing about today. As you know, our aim is to encourage people to think carefully about how technology is affecting the environment and what we can do to help. I'd like to thank the organisers for putting together such a varied and interesting range of seminars for us and all that remains for me to say is – have an informative and enjoyable day and thank you very much for your attention.

 29.2

1 The first point I'd like to make is …

2 I'm in the lucky position of being able to …

3 I'll try to be as brief as I can.

4 Everyone knows that …

5 If you look at the handout, you'll see that …

6 Following on from that …

7 Let's move on.

8 I'd like to finish by saying …

9 It's been a real pleasure …

UNIT 30

 30.1

1 People often don't believe me when I tell them I can remember actually being inside a pram and looking out. I must have been under a year old. It's just a very quick snapshot that I have in my memory. I have this picture of my pram, framed by the edge of a black hood – it must have been raining – and halfway down the picture, going horizontally across, is a spring with brightly coloured balls on it. At the end of my pram is an old toy – a rabbit or a dog, propped up in the corner.

2 I was about nine and we were on holiday in the south of England. We'd gone for a picnic in the countryside, my mum and dad, my sister and me. Mum was sorting out the picnic and Dad was showing my sister some fish in the stream. I wandered off, as boys do, and found a good tree to climb. I was up it in a couple of minutes and I remember very clearly hanging upside down on this branch. Then this weird thought came into my head. Somehow, I knew that there was a big field on the other side of the hedge about a hundred yards away. I knew that there was a big black bull in the field and it had a white collar on. I also knew that there was a dead tree in the middle of the field. I climbed down and ran over to the hedge and looked through. Sure enough, there was the field, the black bull with the white collar and the dead tree!

3 Oh – there are so many instances I can give you. I'm sure it's because we overload our memories but I do get worried sometimes. The most recent was when I was out shopping with my husband and we met a work colleague who I've worked with for five years at least. I was going to introduce them but could I remember his name? It was gone, a complete blank. I felt a total fool. Words too go from time to time. I was talking to a friend about a tennis game and I wanted to use the word 'net' but it wouldn't come. I ended up saying, 'You know, the thing in the middle of the court!'

4 When I was really young there was this fire in a house on our street. I have this vivid memory of flames bursting from the windows and black smoke hanging over the street. I can even smell it. I can also remember the noise of the fire engines and the crowds of people watching. It's only recently that during a conversation with my parents it came out that I wasn't actually there at the time! I was away, staying with my grandparents. Isn't memory a strange thing?

UNIT 33

 33.1

A: Hey, have you read this survey?

B: Which one?

A: It's about people living to a hundred and what they'd give up to live that long.

B: And?

A: Apparently not much! People in general would rather die young after a short happy fulfilling life than linger on in a nursing home in bad health and with no money.

B: Yeah. But if you've still got all your faculties – why not? I know some really sprightly older people.

A: We're talking a hundred!

B: Well, the way we're going with modern medicine and all that, we'll probably still be climbing mountains or whatever when we're a hundred.

A: Yes. That's it, isn't it? Live till you're a hundred or exist. There's a big difference.

UNIT 34

 **34.1**

J = Mr Jessop, **P** = Mrs Parker, **F** = Mr Farlowe

J: Good morning, I'd like to speak to Mrs Parker.

P: Yes. That's me.

J: Good morning Mrs Parker. My name is Ian Jessop. I'm phoning from the International Lottery Agency and I am delighted to inform you that you have just won second prize in the Canadian Lottery for March.

P: But I never entered the Canadian Lottery. You must have the wrong person.

J: No, Mrs Parker. Your name was one of several hundred that were entered randomly. You have won a substantial cash sum. It amounts to £1,000,000 minus insurance.

P: That's amazing! I can't believe it. This isn't a joke, is it?

J: I can assure you that this is no joke. Let me put you through to our accounts department and they will talk you through what happens next and how the money will be transferred to you …

F: Hello, Mrs Parker. David Farlowe here from International Lottery Accounts. I understand congratulations are in order?

P: Apparently. I'm still reeling from the shock!

F: Well, don't worry. I'm here to help you. First I need to take a few details. Is that OK?

P: Sure.

F: Can you give me your bank and account number, please?

P: Is it safe to give out that information over the phone?

F: You're quite right to be careful. I can give you my number and you can call me back to establish that I am who I say I am. Shall I do that?

P: No, that's OK. My bank is National Bank, Account number 012348765.

F: Thank you, Mrs Parker. That is all I need to know. The money should be transferred to your account within a fortnight, as soon as we receive the insurance premium.

P: Insurance?

F: Did my colleague not mention this to you?

P: Oh yes, I think he did say something about insurance but I wasn't really listening.

F: That's understandable. Well, when transferring an amount of money this substantial from Canada, it needs to be covered by insurance. In the case of your prize, the premium will be £250. If you could send us a cheque for this amount, your money will be covered and we'll be able to release it. Is that all right?

P: Fine. It's not much compared to a million pounds is it?

F: Absolutely. And perhaps next time you'll win the first prize of five million! If you could send the cheque to …

UNIT 38

 38.1

The film tells the story of Marion Crane, a young woman who is in love with a guy called Sam Loomis. She embezzles money from her boss so that she and Sam can be together. Marion runs away and ends up at an isolated motel called the Bates Motel which is run by a young man called Norman.

Norman lives with his bedridden mother in an old mansion adjacent to the hotel. Marion takes a room at the motel and over dinner she and Norman discuss life and its traps.

Marion decides to go back and return the money but she doesn't have the chance. That night she is stabbed to death while in the shower by a shadowy figure that looks like an old lady. Norman discovers the body and is horrified. He hides the body and cleans up after the murder to protect his mother.

Other people arrive at the Bates Motel looking for Marion. A private investigator, Milton, comes first and is stabbed on the stairs in the mansion. Then Marion's boyfriend, Sam, arrives with her sister, Lila, and they discover that in fact Norman's mother died several years ago.

While Sam tries to distract Norman, Lila goes to search the mansion. She goes down to the basement where she finds the mummified corpse of an old lady. Meanwhile Norman becomes suspicious and knocks Sam out. He goes up to the mansion. Suddenly 'Mother' comes up behind Lila. Sam arrives on the scene just in time to save Lila and they find that 'Mother' is in fact Norman, dressed in his mother's clothes.

Later at the police station we learn that Norman killed his mother in a jealous rage and since then he has kept his mother 'alive' by taking on her identity. He has shut out any memory of what really happened. The film finishes with Norman alone in his cell.

Published by
DELTA PUBLISHING
Quince Cottage
Hoe Lane
Peaslake
Surrey GU5 9SW
England

www.deltapublishing.co.uk

© Delta Publishing 2009

First published 2009

ISBN 978-1-905085-14-9

Edited by Tanya Whatling
Designed by Christine Cox
Illustrations by John Plumb
Photo research by Emma Bree
Printed by Melita Press

Acknowledgements
We are grateful to the following for providing permission to reproduce copyright material:

The Daily Mail 2003 for extracts from 'Proof that you can read minds', published by *The Daily Mail* 26th April 2003; The Daily Mail 2006 for table of statistics from 'The great British grind', published by *The Daily Mail* August 10th 2006; The Daily Telegraph 2006 for extracts from 'Junk culture is poisoning our children', published by *The Daily Telegraph* 12th September 2006.

The publishers would like to thank the following for their kind permission to reproduce their photographs:

Cover photos: ©iStockphoto.com/Pidjoe, J. F. Mora Soria, Webphotographeer, C. Schmidt.

Inside photos : ©iStockphoto.com/A. Murillo, iofoto, A. Raths, G. Stevense, E. Hart, Hammondovi, M. Sherrill, J. Wackerhausen, I. Stevanovic, Pidjoe, R. Sengupta, K. Binns, R. Wijaya, C. Schmidt, J. Horrocks, A. Fedorov, J. Koch, E. Kubicka, K. Lau, J. Gough, P. Cowan, S. Trigg, L. Janos, R. Frommknecht, A. M. Kurtz, C. Wheatley, S. Witas, L. Banks, Ilbusca, L. Pettet, J. Smith, L. Dodz, P. Genest, Lanciatore, R. Stouffer, I. Habur, F. Anderson, J. Pulispher, Andresr, Tillsonburg, G. Hellier, M. Augustine, C. O Driscoll, Zone Creative, S. Stone, S. Von Niederhausern, A. Kwiatkowski, D. Kneafsey, P. Hermans, V. Prikhodko, Martínez Banús; Nikada, I. Canikligil, S. Srdjanov, J. V. Cantió Roig, J. F. Mora Soria, J. Semeniuk, V. Lebedinski, S. Dominick, L. Valder, Q. Nguyen, R. Lee, P. Berry, Y. Gavryush, T. Temelkov, D. Bishop, Gearhart, J. Pauls, Tomm L, Mr Sailor.

R. Jack/Corbis; Paramount, Dreamworks, Lionsgate/EVT, G. Robinson, S. Clark/Rex Features; E. Bree; S. Reddy, J. Arnold Images/Alamy, S. Barbour, B. Brandt, Hulton Archive/Getty Images.

Lynda Edwards would like to thank Nick Boisseau for believing in the project and Tanya Whatling for her advice and excellent editing. The book also owes a great deal to John Plumb's illustrations.